*M*other*talk*

Mother*talk*

Life Stories *of* Mary Kiyoshi Kiyooka

Roy Kiyooka

edited by

Daphne Marlatt

NeWest Press

First Edition

Canadian Cataloguing in Publication Data

Kiyooka, Roy.
  Mothertalk

  ISBN 1–896300–24–3

  1. Kiyooka, Mary Kiyoahi, 1896–1996. 2. Japanese
Canadians—Biography.* 3. Japanese Canadians—Evacuation
and relocation, 1942-1945.* I. Marlatt, Daphne, 1942- II. Title.
FC106.J3Z7 1997   971'.004956'0092   C97–910586–2
F1035.J3K59 1997

Edited by Daphne Marlatt
Editor for the Press: Robert Kroetsch
Cover and book design: Brenda Burgess
Photographs have been reproduced with the kind permission of the Kiyooka family.

NeWest Press gratefully acknowledges the support received for its pub-lishing program from The Canada Council's Block Grants program, and The Alberta Foundation for the Arts. The Estate of Roy Kiyooka gratefully acknowledges the support received from the Japanese Canadian Redress Foundation for the writing and editing of this book.

Printed and bound in Canada by Transcontinental Printing Inc.

NeWest Publishers Limited
#201, 8540-109 Street
Edmonton, Alberta T6G 1E6

NeWest Press acknowledges the support
of the Multiculturalism Program of
the Department of Canadian Heritage.

To the Issei women of Mary Kiyooka's generation.

Contents

Introduction

The astonishing sweep of "Mary" Kiyoshi Kiyooka's life-story is resonant with the painful displacement of immigration, intensified by Canada's shabby treatment of its Japanese citizens during World War Two. But also, and just as significantly, it is vivid with the spirit of a woman endlessly curious about the vagaries of human existence and grounded, at the same time, in the Bushido code of ethics she learned as a child.

Growing-up at the turn of the century in Tosa (Kochi City), the favoured and feisty daughter of a well-educated samurai, Masaji Oe, who developed the Iai school of swordsmanship, she was expected to marry and perform the conventional roles of unquestioning wife and mother. Unconventional by character and training (she received much the same training as her father's male Kendo-students), she accepted the marriage arranged by her father and, in 1917, found herself sailing to the relatively uncivilized West Coast of Canada to join her emigrant husband. Even as she embraced this adventure, she could not then have anticipated selling vegetables to make ends meet for their large family in Depression-era Calgary, nor could she have imagined themselves being forced out of the city in 1942 to an abject plot of land in northern Alberta which had somehow to be farmed for the family to survive.

And yet this is not just the story of an extraordinary woman. As Mary herself keeps reminding us, she is an Issei, a first-generation Japanese immigrant to Canada. She is keenly aware of belonging to a scattered and now passing community, one that felt the brunt of hostilities against them as "Enemy Aliens." They are a generation of survivors, and she is proud of them, even as she elegizes the hardships they experienced.

Tosa, her "heart's true country," is both a prefecture (Kochi-ken) in the south of the island of Shikoku, and a city (Kochi), the capital of its prefecture. Nudged by the Pacific Ocean at about 33 degrees latitude, Kochi's climate is relatively balmy, its vegetation subtropical. Mary refers to it as Tosa because that was its name under the old feudal system. In fact, the city of Tosa grew up around the castle of the Yamanouchi clan, built in 1603. This is the clan that Mary's father served as a samurai. The Meiji period (1868–1912), the period Mary Kiyoshi Kiyooka was born into, saw the end of the feudal system with the restoration of the Emperor's power as centuries of control by the Shoguns (military commanders-in-chief of the feudal system) were abolished. This change of course brought upheaval as certain samurais, like Ryoma Sakamato, a Tosa hero, fought against the shogunate. Mary's link with this major historical moment reaches back through the vivid memories of her father, who was almost fifty when she was born in 1896. Even her early life was touched by war, the Russo-Japanese War of 1904-5 which took the lives of many of Tosa's young men.

When she was first interviewed for this book, Mary Kiyooka was in her early nineties. She celebrated her 100th birthday in 1996 with a big party in Edmonton and died a few months later. She outlived, by two and a half years, her son Roy Kiyooka, well-known in Canadian painting circles of the

1960s and early 70s for his geometric abstract canvases, an artist who subsequently abandoned his painting career to make photography, writing, and music at the intersection of the Asian and Western cultural heritages he found himself living out. It was Roy, feeling the inadequacy of his own Japanese, who asked his friend, the translator Matsuki Masutani, to interview his mother at length in her mother-tongue and then transcribe and translate her stories into English. The first interviews were done over several days in 1986 in Roy's living room and subsequent ones five years later at the Calgary home of his brother, Harry. Matsuki Masutani recalls Roy laughing about this process, "I need a translator to listen to my own mother's story — what a funny situation I'm in." (personal letter, June 13, 1995) But as Matsuki commented, the communication between Roy and his mother was intimate and transcended the language difficulty between them.

Roy himself has written about the significance of his deep connection with his mother in terms of language: "She and she alone reminds me of my Japanese self by talking to me in the very language she taught me before I even had the thot of *learning* anything. If there's one thing I can say with a degree of certainty, it's that she did not, could not, teach me to speak English. Let alone, read and write it. After more than half a century in Canada her English is, to say the least, rudimentary. Not that that ever prevented her from speaking her mind. So it is that I find myself going home to keep in touch with my mother tongue and, it must be, the ghost of my father's silences." (See Appendix 2,"We Asian North Americanos.")

Once the interviews were transcribed and roughly translated, Roy took Matsuki's pages and freely rewrote them, fashioning a voice in English that would reflect his mother's

Tosa-ben. It was to be his last writing project and, as Matsuki has observed, "Before he passed away, Roy said to me, 'This is my last writing. I wrote everything I wanted to write about' in his Tosa dialect. It must have meant a lot for him to render his lost mother-tongue into English." (personal letter, June 13, 1995.)

In fact, much of what Roy wrote on language for his friends, the writer Joy Kogawa and the photographer Tamio Wakayama, and then delivered at the Japanese Canadian/Japanese American Symposium in Seattle in 1981, prefigures his final *Mothertalk* project. His comments on the period-quality of his own Japanese are particularly relevant: "Everytime I've been in Japan I've been acutely aware of the fact that my own brand of Japanese is previous to both the 2nd W.W. and television. That in fact it's contemporaneous with that original wireless talking machine, the radio. My more candid Japanese friends tell me that I sound to their ears, a bit old-fashioned. Need I say that I didn't have enough of a handle on my mother tongue to tell them that all the Japanese I know had been distilled in me by the time I was six or seven. Keep in mind that my mother's Japanese was shaped towards the end of the Meiji era and the beginnings of the Taisho era and that's the Japanese she taught me. What has been grafted on down thru the years is, like my mother's English, rudimentary." ("We Asian North Americanos.")

What is in no way "rudimentary," is the particular quality of the English he fashioned for the story of his mother's life. A plastic fusion of formality and distinctly colloquial words or phrases, many of them with an out-of-date whiff about them, this language is an English version of the Tosa dialect she acquired as a child at the turn of the century, a dialect arrested in time from the point of her emigration. It is, as he points out, the dialect he grew up speaking, and it influenced the English in which he wrote his own poems, letters, and statements.

After Roy's sudden death in 1994, his daughters, Mariko, Fumiko, and Kiyo, asked me to edit his manuscript for publication. When I read over the pages of transcript and compared them to Roy's last draft, I found that he had considerably expanded many stories, adding vivid detail and sometimes wry social or political commentary that matched his mother's occasional comments in this vein. It's impossible to know whether the detail comes from his own poetic elaboration, sparked by visits he made to Kochi-ken over the years, or whether it comes from other, earlier versions he heard his mother tell.

I also found that Roy's final version had abandoned the chronologically specific nature of the original interviews for a free-floating succession of stories that jumped around in time and place. Factual biographical material had been dropped out and stories were linked thematically or verbally rather than chronologically, sometimes not linked at all, and sometimes repeated elsewhere in the manuscript. All of this left a reader with a sense of immediate experience but no sense of the overall arc of Mary's life. True, we rarely experience our lives as having an obvious line of development in the flux of our actually living them out from day to day. But it's difficult to stay intrigued with the details of someone else's life without having some sense of the emotional weight of those details. And to tell an event in a life so that a reader can feel its weight requires a sense of what has preceded that moment.

It seemed to Matsuki and me that Roy had been working to convey the obsessive return of certain motifs in his mother's version of her life. And perhaps even to suggest the patterning apparent in a life when it is closely looked at. He knew the outline intimately — it was the groundwork for his creative refashioning. But the outline itself is a remarkable story in its own right — as his added commentary serves to point up — and it deserves to be seen clear. So I opted for a more conservative approach and carefully unwove the stories he had rewoven, establishing when each occurred and what it stood in relation to. The transcripts were my guide for chronology, as well as later information generously provided by other family members.

As for sequencing, that was guided by a certain familiarity with the kinds of concerns Roy was dealing with, and a growing familiarity with the way Mary's associations might work. I should admit here that I am not a disinterested editor. Roy and I lived together from 1975 until 1981 and during that time his mother stayed with us on a number of occasions. Our conversation was limited by my almost-complete ignorance of Japanese and her "rudimentary" English, but we nonetheless managed some genuine exchanges. She was passionate in her need to communicate openly with people and tireless in her fascination with others' life-stories. I can only say that some of my sequencing has been simply intuitive, based on this sense of her and of Roy's sense of her as he conveyed it to me. I've wanted his words to stand as he wrote them, though not always in the order which he gave them. I also wanted the stories to retain their oral feel in the way they spin off one another, much as Mary's conversation did. To that end, whenever I went looking for a bridging sentence and couldn't find it in his version, I went back to the transcripts. As a result, there are only a handful of my own linking words within the narrative itself.

The problem was how to reshape the narrative into a chronological movement, yet also sustain some sense of the return of certain motifs, particularly as they revolve around Mary's parting from her father and from Tosa. These regrets have a peculiarly haunting quality, which lingers like an undertone throughout her subsequent life in Canada. One of Roy's favourite words was "abiding" and one of his favourite conversational motifs had to do with "shape," the shape of the lives of people close to him. I felt my work was to clarify the emotional shape of the narrative, its skeletal arc, and yet at the same time keep the surface conversational flow, the quick and various stories about family and friends, the incessant moving back and forth between Canada and Japan.

It should be evident by now that *Mothertalk* cannot be read as documentary. It is a creative retelling that has been carefully worked, a blend of both mother's and son's vision and voices. Even the original material, recorded when Mary was in her nineties, had already undergone subtle transformations of memory over time, altering from lived experience into a form of family legend. We all do this, we constantly retell, to ourselves and others close to us, the story of our lives, and such retelling tends to simplify the inarticulate complexity of original experience into something more clearly formulated as story and remembered as such. In this transformation even the so-called "facts" can shift, which is why different members of the same family will have different accounts of an experience they originally shared. Hence, the occasional footnotes when one or another of Roy's siblings objected to Mary's version of an event that involved them. Hence also the inclusion of her husband Harry Shigekiyo Kiyooka's somewhat different version of early events. (See Appendix 1.) What continues to remain "true," however, is the emotional weight of the story for the teller, and this is what comes through so clearly in the memories told and retold in *Mothertalk*.

Mothertalk is Roy's great gift to his mother and his family, this poignant tracing of the emotional matter of his mother's life and thus the unspoken shaping of his own and his siblings' lives. The interplay of the accidental and the chosen, the purely personal and the massively historical, moving through a life delicately balanced between hope and regret, is his tribute, not only to her individual will to survive the depersonalizing effects of racism, and to survive with intelligence, humour, and ethical values intact. It is also his tribute to the collective will within the Issei community to survive on just those terms the shattering events and prolonged after-effects of World War Two in Canada.

⌐ ⌐ ⌐

Many people have offered me considerable help in this project. My gratitude goes to Matsuki Masutani, first of all, who gave his enthusiastic support and much crucial information on Roy's project, as well as translation and editorial advice. My thanks to Roy's brothers and sisters, particularly to Frank Kiyooka and to Joyce Kiyooka, who generously provided family information, photographs, and other forms of support. Thanks to Roy's daughters: Kiyo who handled the business-end of things, kept in constant touch, and provided the bulk of the photographs; Fumiko who suggested including some of Roy's poems and gave me useful background information on Tosa; and Mariko who first contacted me about doing the book. Thanks to Diane Martin for her encouraging interest in the project.

My appreciation and gratitude to Tony Tamayose and the Japanese Redress Foundation, which donated outstanding funds from an initial grant to Roy for this project, and to Frank for so generously donating the remainder of his own grant.

And thanks to NeWest Press for seeing it into the light of day, most particularly thanks to Smaro Kamboureli and Robert Kroetsch for welcoming the manuscript and providing editorial advice.

Daphne Marlatt
May 1997

$\mathcal{E}$*verywhere he walked that Fall pages out of his past spoke of inchoate presentiments. His mother turned ninety-four that summer. In former years she would sit and knit thick woolen slippers in an array of colors for members of the family while she kept an eye on her favourite soap opera, but this year she did one or the other and as often as not nodded off with the unknit slipper on her lap. They spent long summer evenings together remembering distant 'names' and 'faces' and they recounted the kindred and alien time-warps. Each summer she cited the names of those she knew who had recently passed away, and in her obits she would cite how each of them passed their presciences onto those who were alive and kicking. Her many great grandchildren not the least amongst them. Thus for a month each summer since the early seventies she flew over the mountains to be with him: And though it was never enough to simply sit and knit she would finish a vest for a son or a pair of slippers for a daughter, and when she felt like talking she invariably talked about all the family ties they had on both sides of the Pacific, and though she never mentioned it, they both knew she was the last link to the sad and glad tidings of the floating world. . . .*

from "Pacific Windows" (1990)

Part One

My Heart's True Country

 any Issei I know have told me that when their time comes they want to return to the country of their heart. When we were young and raising a family we didn't have the time to think about such things but now that we're old and death is just around the corner it comes to mind. O I live well enough and I do whatever my old bod lets me do but my true wish is to go back to Tosa one last time.

Seven of my high school class-mates there are alive and well. Two of them go to an old people's college to keep their minds lively. They write to me regularly in a firm hand. At ninety-plus their minds are clear. O let's live to be a hundred without going senile, the frailest one wrote recently.

When Roy and I went to Kochi in the eighties they got together and arranged a reunion at the new Kochi Hotel. Imagine a bunch of old women in their eighties and nineties whooping it up. We laughed and talked and cried and showed each other our family pictures and before we went our separate ways we had our portrait taken. When I got home that portrait was waiting for me. One of them had written on the back, it's too bad that dear Kiyo had to return to Canada but we will always hold her dearly in our hearts.

Well I'm too old to go to Nippon alone and my kids tell me I'm too frail for them to want to take me. They say, Mom you've been lucky, you've been to Japan many times. Many Issei women never got back. Ah that's true I guess and I know I've been lucky that way — but they didn't have a Tosa buried in themselves the way I have. O I've known people who spent their whole lives looking for the place they could call home. Others like me have always known they carry it around inside themselves. Believe me Tosa is my heart's true country.

I don't know how to write English or even make a good sushi but I do know how to knit. I take a nap now and then but only for an hour. I watch the daily news and the soap operas but most of all it's an excuse to sit and knit and when I have a happy thought I put my knitting aside to write to one of my old Tosa friends. My kids will never know all that befell their

Mom because she never learned to speak English well and they didn't learn enough Nihongo.

I've got a thick book that's all about Tosa tucked away in my trunk. It's about famous people like Hirobumi Ito the famous Meiji prime minister and Ryōma Sakamoto whose statue stands on the bluff in Katsurahama Park. There's chapters on the masters of the martial arts and the sword together with Tosa poets musicians famous courtesans. My father Masaji Oe is spoken of as the last great master of the Hasegawa school of Iai and his friendship to the Yamanouchi clan is duly noted. Oh it's chockfull of all manner of things including old wives' tales and folk songs — all that makes Tosa unique. You won't find this book anywhere. Too bad that my kids can't read it. Well, George and Mariko could but they don't care much about the old ways anymore and the others can't.

When I was a child there were lots of haunted houses in our neighbourhood and everyone knew that all manner of things happened in them. For instance someone who usually slept with his head pointing south would get up one morning and to his consternation find his head pointing north. Or the stone lantern near the front entrance would be found one day beside the back stoop. It would be all lit up though it didn't have a wick or a drop of fuel. These kinds of things were common in old samurai houses.

On Obon night I was looking up at the fireworks and from the corner of my eye I saw a wreath-of-fire whirling around the top of the tall pine tree beside our house and I knew then and there that our house was truly haunted. I blinked my eyes in disbelief and when I opened them that fiery blue wreath had vanished. When I told Father about it he nodded his head and said I'm glad you saw it.

We knew we lived in a haunted house because the deed told us that it belonged to a noble samurai family. Local legend said the more notable the family the more likely the house was haunted. But I must say Father didn't really mind that our house was haunted. He didn't mind because he knew how to impale samurai ghosts on the tip of his sword.

Still he went through all the formalities of procurement and called in the Ghost-Catchers to verify that the house was no longer haunted. They in their diligence discovered two moss-covered tombstones under the floor boards on the pine tree side of the house. Ah now you'll be able to sleep unmolested they said gathering up their plumb lines and echo chambers. Father then called in the local gravedigger to unearth the tombstones and had them turned over to the custodian of the local graveyard. To this day I have wondered who the tombstones belonged to and how the house got built on top of them.

One night of the full moon Father and I went off to the Fujinami Shrine to have a better view and looking up at the night sky we saw a wreath-of-fire whirling around the tops of all the pine trees standing beside a haunted house. Nobody knows why these wreaths-of-fire come out of the north but legend tells of how one Lord Yamanouchi was bearing a precious gift homeward when he and his entourage got waylaid by a bunch of bandits up in the North Mountains. The legend tells of how the drunken bandits spat out the liquid from the precious vial-of-longevity after tasting it. And that is why these wreaths always appear out of the north.

Only those who have eyes to see the wreath-of-fire whirling around the top of a pine tree know how to keep the Hungry Ghosts at bay, Father said as we walked home. Ah how the full moon shone after the fiery wreaths burned out.

The city fathers have built a big library and a museum near the Yamanouchi Shrine and the Yamanouchi's once stately residence is now a high-class hotel. Kochi has become a bustling city but in my own mind all the acrimony that lies buried knee-deep in its precincts still haunts my former neighbourhood. I've wondered what Father would think of his beloved Kochi if he were alive.

The Yamanouchis who were the lords of Tosa before the Meiji reformation held my Father in such high regard they gave him a beautiful white horse and all the privileges of their stable. Father was a first class horseman. He also excelled at archery and the long spear and taught these skills to Yodo Yamanouchi one of the three lords of the Edo period. After Yodo-san died his only son who was a bit of a dolt took over and the fortunes of the clan dribbled away. Yodo-san's tomb on Mt. Sitsuzan looks quite forsaken. The Oe family plot with Father's white stake is nearby. I've often wondered if Father and Yodo-san would hail each other across the brow of Mt. Sitsuzan when the full moon shone down on Kochi City.

If you lose your lord and master and hence your stipend and there's nobody empowered to give you a pension what are you going to do to make ends meet? Many samurai became oddballs even beggars and petty criminals. Only those who were cunning enough to marry into the nobility bettered themselves. Western ideas became the craze but most people lived below the poverty line.

We were just a poor samurai family but Father always did what he could for those he met who were in dire need. If there was one shou of rice in the larder he'd give most of it away. Father could put up with his own hunger. He expected us to do the same. But what's more important Father never lost his sense of humour. To have fallen off the back of a gift horse into the trough of poverty was unbecoming without the gift of humour. "Laugh and the world laughs with you. Cry and you cry alone" was his motto.

Of all my kids Roy resembles him most. He has something in line with bushido [samurai code of honour]. The man who is compassionate, who can give away things even when he himself has nothing to eat, is a samurai. My father was one of them.

When I went back to Kochi years ago I met my father's last disciple. He was an honourable Meiji man who had taken it upon himself to see that a commemorative stone got erected in Father's honour. There are no true Iai masters since Master

Oe passed away, but Iai as the way of the sword is alive and well because of him. And that's why I'm only doing my duty, he told me. I didn't have a chance to tell him about my life in faraway Canada but I gave him my blessings and said I would send him every cent I could. That was many years ago.

You see Father was one of the last Edo period samurai with a big heart and much courage and that's why he left the name Oe incised in the annals of Tosa history. And it's odd because his belated fame has made me a small celebrity when I return to Tosa. I must say though, I've really had enough of being treated like an Ojousan [a Miss, as in Miss Oe]. It doesn't fit me at ninety-plus.

For more years than I can count now Father's Iai disciples have wanted to put up this stone in his honour. I've been back to Kochi many times to do what I could on their behalf. The city bureaucrats kept dragging their feet over the land deed so I turned up at City Hall one day to plead with them. I said, All we need is a piece of consecrated ground. The big stone has been inscribed and is lying half asleep in the temple grounds. Please do everything you can to hasten the deed. I won't be around much longer and I would like to see that big stone hold its blunt head up to the sun.

As I've said the samurai found themselves without a master and hence without an income. They'd all been trained to live by their swords and now their swords were only fit for the pawnshop. To make ends meet Father taught martial arts in the local high school and to the local police force. Now my father was one of the luckier samurai because he had several skills. Apart from teaching martial arts he had his moxibustion licence and practised it seriously on his family and friends. Moxibustion really works. It's good for rheumatism neuralgia and stomach pains. It's particularly good for those with cold hands and feet. Father treated us whenever we got ill and outlived his own cancer by treating himself. Look! I still have moxibustion marks on my arm. I'm sure it's one of the many reasons I've lived such a long life.

There was a big age gap between me and my father. He was almost fifty when I was born so I was like a great grandchild for him. In the old days you didn't ask parents about the date of their birth. But he was born before Meiji [1868–1912] in the Kaei Period [1848–54]. At the time of the Meiji Restoration he was around twenty. Young yes but men of those days matured young. Even Ryōma Sakamoto [Tosa hero of the Meiji Restoration] was only about thirty then. It was a different time. A man of thirty was as reliable as a man of fifty or sixty today whether he was a peasant or a samurai. It was Showa 2nd [April 18th, 1926] when he died at the age of seventy-six. I was in Calgary and Roy was only four months old. My brother sent a telegram saying, Come home. I wanted to go but we didn't have any money. He died from the cancer apparently although he had survived it for a long time, thanks to moxibustion.

My brother Mizuho was four years older than me but he was weak and died young. Because my brother didn't have the physical strength my father taught me. If I were a man I wouldn't be here in Canada. I would have succeeded him. But what could I do? I'm a woman. When I was little though I was a tomboy. His way of bringing me up was rather rough though I must say he never spanked me.

In Kochi there was a hall called Butokuden [Hall of Martial Arts]. It was in the park below the Yamanouchi castle. During the war it burned down in an air raid but when I was a child my father taught Kendo and Iai there. I still remember midwinter training. All the young guys would wake at four in the morning and half-asleep they would stumble to the well at the Butokuden and pour cold water on themselves. It's not too cold in Tosa in the winter — just thin ice cover. Then dripping wet they ran back into the dark butokuden to sit upright on their heels until their mind and breath calmed down. At Father's command they rose on wobbly legs and turning bowed to their opponents before drawing their swords with a piercing holler. Under Father's eye all these young guys went through the motions of hand-to-hand combat. And because I tagged along with Father I wielded my small sword with the rest of them. O it's too bad my brother didn't have the strength to be Father's heir. That's why he indulged the tomboy in me.

I'll tell you a story from my youth the story of my childhood honour. When I was around ten the Honourable Itagaki [prominent figure of the Meiji era from Tosa] came to Kochi. He was chief of the Liberal Party and we had a big dinner to welcome him at the Tokugeturo Restaurant. At this party I performed sword-dancing for him wearing the Hakama [traditional pants] and a sword just as my father had taught me.

There's a poem about Shingen's retreat in battle [Takeda Shingen, 1521–73, one of the powerful feudal lords whose struggle with his main rival in Kawanakajima was a favourite subject of poetry and plays]. Father sang the lines — he was an excellent singer — and I danced to it. Honourable Itagaki was delighted. He beckoned me up, Come here, come here, oh what a good child! and patted my head. This is one of my shining memories. When I went back to Tosa I told this story to Father's disciples who were so pleased to hear it. There they were — all about sixty and nodding their heads — Is that so! O is that so!

Today on TV you can see Princess Diana mixing with all sorts of people and they adore her for it. In Tokugawa times those who had pomp and power never acted that way. Common people didn't have much to do with the rich and powerful except as tradesmen and vassals. And everybody knew the pitfalls of going outside of their own precincts. I'm not too sure how class works in Canada where all kinds of people mix freely but I'm sure it's there. Most people want to be different. You don't see bankers hanging around with truck drivers in the local pub. The rich and beautiful never belong to the same clubs as you or I do. Though I was brought up with all the advantages of a samurai's daughter, I've spent my whole life with ordinary people. I don't have any rich friends. I only know such people on TV and I see how charming they can be but they're not the kind of people I'm used to.

My old Kochi friends say they deplore the post-MacArthur generation for making such a big thing out of the Christian

Christmas instead of the Shinto New Year. They haven't got giri-ninjou [proper custom and manners combined with compassion] is their common complaint. I think those born in the ashes of Hiroshima are often spiritually at odds with themselves and I suppose that's why they're workaholics. More and more things don't lead to pleasure let alone happiness.

When the last Issei dies the old values will wither away. Maybe not. I know my values are those my Father taught me and I have just gone on practising them. You can't make up values by yourself and you can't buy them. It's all in the way you act in the world knowing every act is part of the whole fabric. If someone gives you a gift, you give them one in return. You do that from a sense of giri [proper custom]. On the other hand, if a beggar asks you for money, you give him what you can and bless him. That's ninjou [compassion]. Giri-ninjou is the very heart of the samurai's way of life. People nowadays don't seem to exchange gifts in the way they used to. They seem to have misplaced the meaning of gratitude.

My generation keeps it up. Whenever I go to Nippon I always take herring roe and kelp for my old Tosa friends. If I don't they'll think Master Oe's daughter has misplaced her giri-ninjou. Ha. Look at my kids — they go to Japan all the time but nobody expects them to bring gifts. Surely life itself is the first gift — doesn't that make gift-giving meaningful?

When my son Harry and I went to Kochi many years ago, I showed him the house I grew up in and I showed him where I used to play beside the Otagawa. I was born below Kochi

Park just one cho away from the Yamanouchi family residence. At the turn of the century most of the homes in the area belonged to samurai and their kin. There were no shops nearby. It was my neighbourhood and I knew it as well as the back of my hand. It's odd but in all the years I have lived in Canada I've never got to know a neighbourhood as well as my childhood one.

My paternal grandparents lived in a Kochi suburb about an hour from home. My brother and I used to visit them on weekends. We knew they would be pleased to see us and they always had a treat for us. After listening to our small adventures and how we were doing at school they would give us a copper coin and send us on our way. Now Meiji coins were heavy. You knew you held something solid in your hand. Each coin was worth two cents and with two cents we could buy four cookies. So on our way home we would drop into a bake-shop and get rice cookies to munch on. Remember there were no cars then. Nothing to run you down except hand-drawn carts.

There's a bridge named Ryukou-bashi in the east end near Mount Godai. On the far side of the bridge there was an island that used to be the prostitutes' quarters. You could see their washing fluttering from their balconies on the boat to Tanezaki. By the time I left Kochi a brand new bunch of politicians decided that the red light district was an eye-sore and they cleaned it up. I don't know where the prostitutes went but I'm sure they have a new address just around the corner. As long as there are men without women and women without incomes there'll always be a prostitutes' quarter. Ryukou-bashi is still the same bridge though the river is just a trickle full of junk. Everything that was once fabulous and familiar has gone. Everything but venerable Mount Godai.

O it's too bad Harimaya-bashi is just a muddy trickle now. When I was a kid I would stand on my tiptoes to peer over its railing at the orange and gold carp swarming below. The water was so clear you could see all the shining pebbles lying on the bottom. But what I remember most is the lovely sight of candle-lit paper lanterns floating on the river on Obon night.

In the Meiji era Harimaya-bashi used to be the centre of all kinds of noodle sake and gift shops. Now it's mostly tall face-less buildings. You know Harimaya-bashi is also the name of one of Kochi's famous love songs. It's the bridge on which the ill-fated lovers had their last parting. I used to sing it when I was a high school girl and even today it can bring tears to my eyes.

I graduated from girls' high school in Taishou 3rd [1914]. We may have been poor, but we had education. In Kochi they all sent their kids to school, even the poorest. It was different in Kanagawa, in Osaka, even Tokyo, where they set their kids to work as soon as they reached a certain age. Kochi people thought it important to give their children education.

My father studied in Terakoya [Temple Hall] where boys used to go for their education. Because of the Terakoya the literacy rate in Japan at the end of the Edo Era was higher than in any other country in the world. When the Meiji era came he said he needed to study some more so he studied on his own. His writing was impressive too. In his spare time he put together a unique brush-pen with a handle shaped from young pine that the nearby mountain people supplied him with. His pen was named Senzaikan by Saskai Nobutana a famous poet of the Meiji era who sent him a poem inscribed with one of them. Father was moved. He wanted to start a cottage industry but he didn't have the means so he made a small shop in front of the house for his brush-pens and other writing materials.

When Father enrolled me in public school he wrote sizoku [samurai class] as our status in the school register. When I enrolled George and Mariko I entered them as heimin [commoners] because they belonged to the Kiyooka side of the family. Well into the Meiji period the Kiyookas would have had to bow if a samurai like my father passed by. In those days the class you were born into defined your political status. And so even disenfranchised samurai had an advantage over ordinary people although they too were poor. I know class doesn't seem to count for much nowadays when all sorts of people mix but I think class persists. People like to tout their differences.

My husband came from a mountain village eight li [about twenty-four kilometres] inland from Aki. You follow the Yasuda River till you come to Aki. Then you go up into the mountains on a winding road til you arrive in Umagi-mura. On the mountainside where he grew up the farmers bought their fish from a fish-pedlar who came to the village by toro [dog cart]. Now these carts had large wooden wheels and thick boards laid across them. On these boards there was a wooden trough full of iced fish. The whole thing was covered with gunnysacks and straw. When it was used to haul people you sat on the boards. When I married my husband we went the eight li to Umagi with all the wedding gifts by dog cart. Poor dog! The mountain road was steep and rough. There were two small mountains on the way from which you got a view of the whole Pacific. O I've not forgotten that view or that rough trip. It must have been an omen for what lay ahead for me.

Tosa people don't use a kotatsu [coal brazier foot warmer]. We seldom wore underwear in the old days. Even on those rare winter nights when it got cold enough to freeze there'd only be a thin skin of ice on the Otagawa. Tosa has orange groves, palms, exotic birds and snakes, plus the midsummer typhoons. Now the village my husband came from was only a few hours up into the mountains but those few hours sure made a world of difference. In Umagi it got so damp you could see your breath. And you felt sort of hemmed in by the bamboo-grove mountains. And all this just a few hours from Kochi. I think geography has a lot to do with who we are. My nature is mostly sunny. His could be often glum.

In the Tokugawa days the Kiyooka men were village head-men. They belonged to the class just below the samurai and didn't have to kow-tow to anybody. But by the time I arrived in Umagi as a young bride all that was left of the family estate was the old family house and a small patch of ground around it. My husband's father had a weakness for women and sake and he had squandered the family paternity on a wily woman in a nearby town.

Papa never forgave his father. Even on his death-bed he was adamant. Oi don't send my ashes back to Umagi was his admonition. I being the dutiful wife did as I was told but I asked the crematorium man to save me Papa's nails and a lock of his hair which I put in an envelope. I put that envelope in my purse along with my passport and returned to Umagi. There I slipped it into the niche in the back of the tombstone his family had erected on his behalf. In such meagreness Papa presides over once familiar rice fields sloping away from the old family home. Like the unseen wind ruffling the bamboo slopes behind that old house a whole lifetime brushed my cheeks as I stood there and I could see myself again as a young bride the afternoon I arrived in Umagi-mura.

I guess you could say that my fate began to unravel when my well-meaning father made his big mistake: You see he thought that Papa belonged to the Kiyooka clan in Akaoka who were prosperous farmers and not the Kiyookas of Umagi who were just plain farmers. He never intended me to marry a country bumpkin without any patrimony. O I know this will sound crazy to you but the marriage had been arranged through a marriage-broker and as everyone knows marriage-brokers didn't really care who married who they only cared for their commission. Ruefully Father blessed our marriage and hoped for the best.

I knew a kindly woman who came here as a picture-bride about the same time as I did. She told me that when she first met the eyes of the man who became her husband she didn't like what she saw but as she continued to stare into his unflinching eyes she realized there was no turning back and so she said yes. Their marriage turned out well. They had six kids and lived a long useful life. Towards the end she found she had bone cancer. When I went to see her in the hospital all she could say was, O let my ashes be returned to my mountain prefecture. At the end she had nothing else on her mind. I know how she felt. I've spent most of my life here but Tosa's my real home.

In the beginning Papa's Umagi dialect sounded coarse to my ear. His older sister always said Maa Iyacha [abbreviation of Maa Irashai, your visit is very welcome] whenever she greeted me. My oldest son George talks that way [because he spent his childhood in Umagi]. He doesn't have a lot to say but when he does talk he can sound gruff. Mariko is the only one who speaks proper Japanese. My she's so proper she thinks she can take exception to my Tosa-ben. People in Kyoto [where she lived] think they're the cultivated ones who speak a proper Japanese but to my ears they sound like brittle rice paper. One in a while when I meet a Tosa person I catch myself using slang. We both know what it stands for and get a big kick out of it. But O to tell the truth I've lost some of my Tosa-ben. If you don't speak and hear it daily it lies under your tongue. Sometimes I get all mixed-up and break into English and say "fish" instead of "sakana" — that kind of thing. Ha. I'm sure when I go back to Umagi they'll still greet me with Maa Iyacha. And I'll probably say, YES it's sure been a long while.

All our married life Papa called Oi [hey!] when he wanted my attention. He never called me Kiyo and I never called him Shigekiyo. All our married life we never called each other by our given names. In Tosa your given name wasn't important even after marriage. I came to call him Papa. O it's a good thing the way we call to each other doesn't change from day to day — I mean it would be too confusing. Even today many years after he passed away I still can't say Shigekiyo when I want to talk to him. And I suppose he still thinks he can summon me by simply hollering Oi. I guess all of us are the products of a naming we could never make up.

I went to Primary School for four years to Middle School for four more followed by four years of Women's High School. I wasn't a keen student. I didn't think I could find the world in books. We were taught local History Western Math and World Geography along with all the household skills. We weren't taught any English because it wouldn't be useful to us after we got married. In my time if you weren't pledged to a man by the time you were twenty your chances of a good marriage dwindled until your parents began to treat you like a middle-aged spinster. Nonetheless I'm proud to say we Meiji women are the first modern women. We were the first to graduate from high school and go out into the wider world.

Years later, after I had gone to Edmonton a letter came from Boston out of the blue. It was from Hirita-san who used to live next-door to us in Kochi when he was a boy. I would fight him all the time in Jinjou [elementary school]. I was a real tomboy when I was small and I wasn't afraid of boys. One of his classmates went to see him in America and they talked about old friends. Hirita-san was shocked to learn what had happened to me so he wrote. He was a modern man a painter. He was running an art-shop in Boston where he had lived for a long time but in his old age he wanted to return to Tosa. His family didn't want to live in Tosa so he left them with their consent and returned at the age of seventy. I met him when I went back a few years ago. He was bent over and bald but his face was familiar. O we were so glad to see each other we cried our heads off. We had a good time in the tea shop and had our picture taken. When we parted he said, This might be the last time we see each other. Much of the time I'm flat on my back. Please look after yourself and be happy in Canada. Hirita-san was a true Meiji man who had forsaken his American citizenship and returned to Tosa to die.

My brother went to the first Western-style high school in Kochi and my husband to the second one in Aki. They were taught English by Methodist missionaries who arrived in Admiral Perry's wake. By the time I was born these missionaries had their own churches and a small but faithful following. You see the craze for Western ideas and things took root during the Meiji era.

Now since ancient times Shinto has always been our native religion and Tosa the home of Ten Thousand Gods. The very thought of one god presiding over everything was hard for us to grasp. If you practised Shinto you believed there were as many gods as there are worldly creatures. I know I'll always be Shinto. I sort of lost interest in the missionaries after I left for Canada but my Tosa friends tell me that the idea of one god really caught on and that Christian marriages were all the rage.

When I was a child I knew a woman who became Christian. She was strange — she had one good eye to spy with and one blind eye to see inside things with — but she was always good to me. When the American missionaries came to Kochi she became a Christian. There were very few Christians in Kochi in those days so that made her a rare bird and her family didn't like it. They did everything they could to talk her out of her pledge but they soon realized she had an iron will and wouldn't budge. So they began to bully her. Prodded on by his zealous wife who all along wanted the old one-eyed one out of her sight the son turned against his mother. They made her sit on the tatami and they beat her. One night while she slept he burst into her room and tied her hands and feet up and carried her off to the woodshed. There in a frenzy of name-calling he kicked and beat his mother till there wasn't any breath left in her.

I hadn't seen the old one-eyed woman for a while and I knew nothing about her fate till her bedraggled son showed up at our front door one day with a gunnysack full of junk. Father and I were shocked to see his appearance. There's something uncouth going on was all Father said as he showed him to the door. Several days later he showed up again with his gunnysack full of junk as if nothing untoward had taken place. And as before he took each piece of junk from his gunnysack and presented it to Father as if it were a precious object. Then he asked Father how much he would give him for his gunnysack full of oddments. Needless to say Father found the occasion infuriating and told him not to darken our door again. We thought we were finally rid of him but a few days later there he was again looking as if he had slept in his tatters and had used his gunnysack for a pillow. Father concluded the guy had become a lunatic and made arrangements to have him taken to the local insane asylum. But that wasn't the last of him.

A few weeks later we heard from an asylum guard that he had peeled the skin off his penis and cackling with pain had hung himself from an overhead rafter. When his wife was informed of his hanging she ran out of the house as if her whole body had been set on fire and leapt into the midnight Otagawa. You see in the old demon-tales the Spirit of the Wronged One always comes back in the guise of an Onibaba to enact a Holy Vengeance. Thus with her last breath the old one-eyed one had cast a spell over the two of them for their stupidity. The last time I was in Kochi I got a bouquet of flowers for her grave. She doesn't lie with the rest of the family. She lies apart in her own plot with a small white cross.

Burning Leaves

I am sitting here
              sun on my back
              Autumn in the air

              leaves are falling here
              and over there, over there

I know where I am
my feet stretched out in front of me
still, a part of me is over there

              where leaves are falling
              falling in the Autumn air

              tomorrow there will be bonfires
              people will be burning leaves
              falling leaves will fall into the fire

I am still sitting here, and she
well she, is over there, both of us
watch falling leaves carried away on the inswept air.

              o mother
              where is the rake?

from *Kyoto Airs* (1964)

Part Two

No Notion of What Was in Store for Me

e've had an Old Timers' Club in Edmonton since the fifties. It's odd but those in their sixties don't get along that well with the seventy and eighty year olds. They're mostly Niseis. O they pay their membership fees but they don't come to our meetings. They aren't interested in us oldies. Some of them have never been to Japan, others can only speak a bit of nihongo.

We have had a number of oldies pass away lately — you could say we're an exclusive sort of club and getting more that way with each passing day. I'm the only one left from Tosa. The others hail from Hiroshima, Kumamoto, Sendai,

Kagoshima, Osaka and Fukuoka. We have our funny
moments because nobody wants to admit they're going deaf.

The last one to top ninety recently passed away. Those of us
who are left know our time is running out but we still have
our memories and some of us still enjoy a good conversation.
Others don't have much to say but they're good listeners if
they can stay awake. The men are more bent and older looking. They don't like to talk about the past — I guess they've
all got empty heads.

One old guy who used to drop in on us had a good head.
He came from Kyushu in his youth and had been a fisherman on the West Coast. I told him I had lived in Victoria as
a young bride and knew about the fishermen who came to
town to get drunk and fool around with the prostitutes and
how the owner of the Oda Hotel went back to Nippon at the
end of the season with a fat wallet. With a big grin on his
face he asked how come I knew all this.

I told him how it came home every night in the guise of a
drunken husband who gambled all night with the guys and
nearly lost his shirt not to mention his penis. He was so
happy that someone still remembered those days he bawled
his head off. We agreed to meet again but he never came by.
All of us Issei are dying off like summer flies.

O I've dreamed of performing Sigin [singing recitation of
Chinese-style poems] for the Old Timers' New Years Party but
I've always held back because they would simply yawn and

say Kiyooka-no-oba is showing off again. Nisei and Sansei wouldn't understand it at all. I wouldn't mind performing Iai for somebody who knew the art but I don't have a sword. I guess I could even use a broom handle if the movements were exact. It was an awful loss when my brother wrote to say that he had sold off Father's swords. He should have told me he had to sell them. I could have raised the money to buy them for my sons.

My poor brother used to get drunk when he could afford it and vent his anger on the local prostitutes who then reported his surly ways to the police. When the police found out Mizuho was the sodden son of Master Oe they scolded him and had an officer escort him home. Imagine Father's outrage when the policeman handed him over. Apparently his drinking got worse after I left for Canada. O my brother was a rotten egg but he was a dutiful brother who wrote regularly. I guess it was our way of sharing in each other's miseries. The poor guy lost his wife and then his favourite son.

But his other son is alive and doing well in Siga prefecture. Sumio is like a Bushi, very independent and self-reliant. He's a long-distance hauler who lives in a splendid new house with his wife a pair of twin daughters and several cages full of stray dogs and cats. Awhile back he invited me to one of his twin's wedding. I wrote him, It's really too bad I can't be there but my spindly legs can barely hold me up. From the pictures he sent I could see it was a gala wedding. It must have cost him a small fortune. The young bride was wearing a tsumo-kakushi [bridal hood] to hide the horns of jealousy. What a funny custom! I didn't wear one of those when I got married. We didn't do that sixty years ago.

It was my father's mistake to send me to Canada. No not his mistake. He just thought about me too much. To this day I know I had his unswerving affection. My mother let Father look after me. It was always Father who took me to the public bath and he was the one who would cut my hair. Mother took care of my brother. When she passed away I prayed for her well-being but I didn't cry even though I knew what she had gone through. But when Father passed away I got depressed for a long while and though I kept my depression hidden from the family part of me withered away.

My mother was a quiet person. My father could be gruff. Whenever he got drunk and lost his temper she pretended not to notice and went about her chores. She never talked back. It was just commonsense. After all there was no point taking exception to a drunk man. I've caught myself doing the same thing. What gets passed on from mother to daughter is hard to name but it does have something to do with all the things we have to do in our waking life.

There is an interesting story about their marriage. She lived in the countryside about ten li [forty kilometres] from Kochi City. She was the daughter of a wealthy farmer and reputedly a pretty girl. In the old days samurai used to wear their swords all the time. So one day Father and his friend went to the farm to ask for her threatening to kill them if they refused. She was really scared — she was sixteen then. Mind you sixteen wasn't so young in those days. It would be the same as twenty-five or six now. They were wealthy farmers and of course they didn't want to give her to my father but they couldn't refuse him. Nobody wanted to die my mother told me. As for my father he would tell this story all the time. He was a rough samurai but he was never rough with me.

Father loved his sake and sashimi and I got to fetch it for him. Most of the time he could afford two gou [one gou is .18 litre]. He didn't sit down to savour it no, he drank it up in a single gulp. When he had extra money he got two shou [one shou is ten gou] and downed it in a couple of gulps. Some like to trickle it down their throats, others like a fast scald Father would say wiping his lips on his kimona sleeve. Once when I went out to fetch his sake I mischievously got a bottle of vinegar instead. I loved licking it and licked it all the way home. By the time I got to our street I felt giddy. Father smelled the vinegar on me. He knew what I was up to and putting on his most scornful face he gave me a smack on the bum and said Don't do that again or I'll make you swallow the whole bottle. Then he dipped into his change purse and put a coin in my palm and told me to fetch his sake.

It's odd what one remembers but in the end that's all one has. He had a beautiful voice. Sometimes when he got drunk the old songs sang through him.

In Tosa everybody ate fresh fish and drank lots of sake. But whenever a big typhoon kept the fishermen from setting their nets and there was no fish in town then we bought meat. We couldn't afford the good cuts so we got meat-ends and cooked them with vegetables in a kind of stew. Otherwise it was a bowl of rice a grilled fish with sour pickles and all of it washed down with sake. Tosa has always been famous for its sashimi and sake. Ask any Japanese. I never tasted milk till I came here. Even today I don't care for the taste of it. I guess it's the same as my white friends who don't like the taste of tofu. How things taste must be a deep thing because it sure doesn't leave a trace in the air.

It was always the two of us — Father and me — who went on evening strolls together. On a hot summer night we would walk to the Fujinami Shrine [where the Yamanouchis are buried]. Now there's an ancient pine tree that towers above its stone embankment and one night we came upon a body, a slender body hanging from its branches. Under the tree's spreading night-shade Father and I stood hand in hand looking up at the dangling figure with its tongue hanging out until the police from the local precinct arrived and ran up a ladder to cut the body down. We didn't stay. I was just a child but I could plainly tell the hanged man we saw was just a young guy. Father and I didn't have a word to say on our way home. What could we say to allay that reproachful tongue?

When I was young we were taught geography but we weren't taught much about distant people and places. And though we were neighbours we didn't learn much about the Chinese Okinawans or Koreans except how different they were from us. I guess you could say Tosa was still wrapped inside its feudal cocoon.

I remember the Russo-Japanese War. I was eight or nine. We walked all over Kochi to celebrate the victory after Ryojun finally fell. I sat up high above the crowd on my father's shoulders waving my paper lantern while all around us the townspeople lifted their chochin [lanterns] and shouted BANZAI! BANZAI! There was a drunken joy in the air of Tosa that night! We lived near the park and at the height of the war all the country people gathered there to share one last obento [box-lunch] with their departing sons. We let some of them eat their farewell sushi in our back yard and I served them tea. They were all in good spirits saying Ittekuru-yo [I am going]. Then all those barely trained young men left for the front. Tosa's Forty-Fourth Regiment was wiped out. The Awa Regiment lost every man. Afterwards the military called it a major victory for god and country. That a generation of young men ended up as cannon-fodder didn't matter to them.

When I graduated from high school I wasn't very interested in men though I was the right age for marriage. Even though I knew I wasn't a real beauty I knew I wasn't just plain-looking either. Because I was well educated there were a number of men young and old who wanted my hand. Father turned them all down. He couldn't see me married to a middle-aged merchant with his mistresses and the life of a doctor's wife would be too boring for a lively person like me he said. What you need is an adventurous man. Someone to match your audacity. I'll miss you but I think you ought to go abroad. I didn't fantasize about marriage or living abroad. Tosa was enough for me.

Father always believed that America and Canada too was a place where women were treated better. He should have known there weren't many women abroad. But wanting only my happiness he decided I ought to go to Canada where I'd have a chance to make my own life. I thought he must be right. Yes it would be nice, that freedom.

Now all through high school Papa had excelled in his studies and the martial arts. In Meiji times the top students wore gold braids on their caps. Papa had five gold braids. He had been in Canada for years, he was already a worldly guy. Father heard about him through an old samurai friend who had been Papa's martial arts teacher. Father and this friend had been disciples of the same warrior-monk and had fought side by side in the last pitched battles of the Edo period. It was this guy who informed Father that a brilliant student and practicioner of the martial arts had returned home to find himself a wife. Father's old friend hinted he could do a lot worse than have his daughter marry one of his bright students and thus gain himself a son-in-law who would carry on the art of Iai. So Father took the hint and got in touch with the local marriage-broker.

No doubt he was thinking Ah this must surely be the young man I've been searching for, the very one I can pass the secret of Iai on to and what's more he's bright enough to be a match for my daughter. Mind you I'm putting words in his mouth but I tell you that's how I got pledged. He was convinced Papa had it in him to succeed in the New World and that we would return with a pocket full of gold to take up our filial duties. But the truth was that neither Father nor I had any notion of what would be in store for me when I went off to a foreign country.

You see Papa was in Canada because he had had a big quarrel with his feckless father and though he was the eldest son he left home. He not only left Umagi-mura behind he left Nihon for good. He borrowed money from his aunt and sailed from Yokohama. He was heading for California where his friend was doing very well running a big farm. He was planning to go there to study but a storm came up and kept the ship from docking in Seattle. It came to Victoria instead and that's where Papa got off to begin his life in the New World. He was eighteen and he lost himself among the drunkards and gamblers. He had to work like the others getting a job here and there at the railway or as bellboy at a hotel. It's a pity. He had a good brain — by the time I arrived to join him his English was very good.

Down through the years his family pleaded with him to come home but Papa had long ago planted his roots in Canada. I knew about Canada but only on the map. I wasn't interested in it at all. Life is so extraordinary.

My miai [arranged meeting] wasn't very much. I was taken to the local theatre and had a good seat on the main floor. Meanwhile Papa sat with the matchmaker in the balcony. They could see me by peering down but I couldn't see them without turning and looking up. And that's how Papa first caught sight of me.

The first time I saw Papa I thought is that what happens to a guy after he's been living in Canada for ten years? He was sporting a tweed cap and a cigarette was dangling from his mouth. I had no idea what kind of a guy he was and I really didn't find out until I joined him in Canada. Let's say it wasn't love at first sight. Love where we came from was something like the icing on a cake. It wasn't the real cake.

During all our years together Papa never spoke my given name. He never called me Kiyo and I never called him Shigekiyo, which was a mouthful anyway. I called him Anata [intimate form of "you"] until George was born then he became Papa and Papa has been his nickname ever since. O it wasn't in our power to change the rules of the mating game. We lived by the old proprieties.

We were complete strangers. There was no courtship nothing like that. We met briefly a few days after he had looked me over at the theatre and he said if we got married we would go live in Canada. Either way he said I'll be going back to Canada soon because Tosa is no longer home to me.

I was too harried by the thought of getting married to tell him that a part of me felt excited and a part of me felt reluctant. Now I know why. All in all I've had a meagre life and it was mostly because Papa and I simply went on abiding each other for our kids' sake. Our own lives didn't count for much.

Anyhow the day after the theatre performance the marriage-broker took me aside and in no uncertain words said Look despite his humble origins your husband-to-be has many abilities. He can read and write in English and Japanese and he's an adroit practitioner of the martial arts. We know he hasn't saved much money for all the years he's been away but there's no doubt in my mind that he will make his fortune one day.

I had to pretend I was the reluctant bride because the proprieties called for it but I didn't need convincing. I had already made up my mind.

After the wedding I went from Kochi to Yasuda through Aki by toro [dog cart]. I tell you seventy years ago life was primitive. After a while we felt sorry for the dogs so we left the toro on the way and changed to jinrikisha [rickshaw].

They still have dogfights like they used to in Tosa. To see one you have to go to Katsuruhama where there's a big dog-fighting arena. Now these sturdy dogs are bred to be vicious killers but they don't let them kill. When one of them draws blood the fight's over. It doesn't last very long but the rage to kill sends a chill up your spine. After the fight you can see them cooped up in their steel cages their breath panting ears chewed up and eyes glazed over. It's the kind of blood sport macho men in Shikoku have always taken pleasure in. Cock fights used to be very popular in Tosa. They were also swift and bloody and usually ended in a dead bird. I saw these shows when I was young. That's why I'm different from those women who would faint at the sight of a drop of blood.

I stayed in Japan for a year after I got married. Those days that was the regulation. After I became a member of the Kiyooka family I had to wait a year to join him in Victoria. Papa's father was a gruff sort of guy who often picked on his wife. He did this while I was in Umagi. He didn't pick on me because I was a samurai's daughter and the new bride in the house. I didn't say much. I pretended to be obedient. I felt sorry for his wife but I was determined I wouldn't put up with such abuse. Still you can pick on these old women but you can't knock them down. They're like those Russian dolls with bright red aprons and round bottoms. You can shove them around but you can't push them over. My own mother was the same way. Obedience doesn't mean you don't have your own mind. I got smarter as the years passed, I learned how to save myself. But more important I always had my own thoughts.

My mother wouldn't think of talking back particularly to her husband. Even when she knew what his rage was about she'd keep quiet and go about her chores. I guess I was brought up that way. I don't like squabbles either. Whenever Papa got angry I always kept my distance. Of course I got furious with him, I wanted to rage at him for his drinking but I usually kept quiet and hid the bottle. I didn't want to be caught in his derelict pride because I knew that both of us would suffer. Drinking was a big problem among Issei men. Most of them didn't have a woman to comfort them here let alone a family. I guess they drank to assuage their loneliness.

Papa was the quiet type. If I heard him say anything over breakfast I wouldn't expect to hear from him again till suppertime. Even when we were in the living room together he never had much to say. We hardly ever laughed together and seldom went anywhere as a couple. Most of the time Papa would go out by himself. He didn't care much for company unless it was one of his drinking buddies. On the other hand I liked having lively people around me. Papa wasn't one of your nasty drunks. He never got rough with me and beat me up though I know some of his drinking buddies did because their women told me. No Papa's way was to get drunk and when he had had enough he would fall into sweet oblivion.

Because my parents did everything for me I didn't know how to cook rice till I came to Canada. Papa didn't complain about my cooking. He ate anything I put in front of him. But if he wanted to taste mutton he would bring it home and take over the kitchen. You see he had acquired a taste for Western spices which I've never learned to use. I'm just a boil 'em or fry 'em sort of cook. By the time the kids grew up they sure knew their mom was a lousy cook. But there were no other cooks around so they didn't dare complain.

Whenever Papa got drunk he'd turn to the guy beside him and say You're lucky you know, it isn't every guy who's got a wife who knows the true way to a man's heart is through his stomach. My wife doesn't know that. She can't even cook a pot of rice the same way twice. One day it's too dry the next it's wet and gooey. Ha ha ha. He would laugh at his own joke but we knew he was really pointing the finger at me.

In his own eyes Papa failed his kids because he never made enough money to help them with their education. He wanted them to be educated. He could see that educated people had a freedom he never had and he wanted that freedom for his kids. Thousands of Asian men of his generation had heard about "Gold Mountain." He knew about it but like so many Issei he couldn't see the gold under his feet because he kept looking for it over the next horizon.

When I arrived in Canada he was working in the club beside the Empress Hotel. He got the job because he spoke good English but he wasn't the kind to take orders from others. Nonetheless he stuck it out to keep himself in liquor. I didn't know he was on his way to becoming a drunkard. He had been just twenty when he arrived and now he was going on thirty and things hadn't worked out for him. Lots of Issei men were like that.

When I was a young woman it was a big deal leaving Kochi. People wept as if they would never see you again. Going off to Canada was beyond their wildest dreams. But I didn't feel like that because I had already made up my mind by marrying Papa. So I stood waving to Father as the big ocean liner pulled out of Kobe harbour. Back then it took a whole day to get to Kobe. Between Kochi and Awa the ferry boat passes the Muroto Peninsula which is famous in Tosa history for its many shipwrecks but the afternoon I left the sea was perfectly calm. Father who had accompanied me said that he would be the first to catch a glimpse of me from Sitsuzan when I returned to Kochi. That was the big promise — that we would return. I didn't know how far away I was really going. I was twenty. No one told me how huge the Pacific Ocean was. As one day followed another I wondered if I'd ever see land again. Being seasick didn't help. But I survived and one beautiful morning I could see Vancouver Island on the horizon. It felt like we had been at sea for years.

There were many picture brides aboard that ocean liner. O it must have been a sight for the men waiting on the dock. The women all dressed up in their best kimonas some of them holding bright paper umbrellas above their heads to ward off the sun. You could say they were as excited as a flock of geese that bright summer afternoon the big liner docked in Victoria. Now most of them couldn't speak any English at all. They had never used a fork and knife and never sat on a Western toilet. I was one of only three who were married beforehand and we knew our husbands on sight. But the picture brides just had a photo of the guy they were pledged to and so they searched the faces on the dock for the man who looked just like the one in the picture they clutched in their hands. They would ask my husband Is that him Mr. Kiyooka? And he would reply No no he is too young, that older fellow is him. Then they would be shocked — Oh no! — and refuse to marry. As it turned out a lot of the pictures were plainly false. One old guy had sent a picture of himself as a young man. Other plain-looking ones had sent a picture of a good-looking friend. And though most of the brides didn't know it most of the men were just scraping by.

I played the part of big sister to a country girl from Matsuyama. Her parents had come to Kobe to see her off and asked me to take care of her. I didn't mind because we liked each other and soon became confidantes. When we landed in Victoria this middle-aged guy came up to her and held her picture up beside her face and said Aha so you're the one. She was so taken aback by the sight of him she turned away and told him to leave. She was only eighteen and he was at least twenty years older than his photo though it was plain to see he had the same wry smile. I felt sorry for both of them and because she was like my kid sister I let her stay with me. She cried and cried and kept saying Obasan it isn't him, he is different from this picture, I don't want to I don't want to. One thing was perfectly clear — there was no way she could go back to Matsuyama. I felt responsible so next morning I persuaded her to meet the old guy and have a heart-to-heart talk. After all I reminded her she had nothing to lose but her virginity. She said she didn't want to see him again but in the end she consented and as things turned out they got married and it proved to be a good match. They had several kids and lived long useful lives. In the end they were among the lucky ones because so many picture-marriages proved to be an impossible match.

One woman I befriended said no to the burly guy who came up the ramp to claim her. He was a brusque sort of man who didn't take kindly to those who said no so he picked her up and carried her off like a sack of rice. Imagine how she felt being carted off with all those people standing about. Anyhow she didn't want a thing to do with such an uncouth guy so she ran away as soon as she could and came to our place. Now he knew she would show up at our place so he came into town and hung around across the street with a hand gun. He was furious because he had sent his hard-earned money to her to come. He went sort of crazy saying I will kill her if she doesn't listen to me. We were terrified of what he might do. Finally my husband took the gun away from him and let her go with him. Apparently he tied her up in the house. O he was a desperate man — but she was desperate too. She ran away to the women's home a place for women who wanted to escape from their men. She didn't have any decent clothes with her so I gave her my nice kimono.

There was lots of misery with photo-marriages when I came to Canada. I couldn't stand seeing it. Another picture bride I met told me her mother had died of consumption. In those days if a member of your family died of consumption it was like a big black mark on the family and no man would ever think of having you for a bride. That's why she came to Canada as a picture bride. Anyhow she was so upset when she saw the old geezer she was pledged to she tore his picture into shreds right under his nose and told him to leave because she wouldn't have a thing to do with such an old fool. Well I got her a room at the Oda Inn where Asian immigrants stayed until they left for other parts of B.C. and I told her to get a good night's rest and think about her plight. Next morning we met over breakfast and I said to her that it's too bad there's such a big gap in your ages but I tell you he's a nice guy and I could see by the twinkle in his eyes he's fond of you so why don't the two of you get together and talk it over? Well later that day they came by to tell me yes, they were going to get married. At first they lived in Duncan where he worked as a miner. They had a big family. The last time we heard from them it was just before Pearl Harbour. They had moved to Mission where like her mother she died of consumption. Her life wasn't easy but I'm sure she would agree it was a lot more than she would have had in Nippon. Both of us knew that.

When I came there were only a few of us on board who had the requisite fifty dollars to prove we wouldn't be indigent in Canada. As you can imagine fifty dollars was a lot more than most of us had seen let alone held in our hands. So it was agreed between us that we would take our place in the immigration line with our passports in hand and that we would pass the same fifty dollars from hand to hand through our kimona sleeves. My knees were shaking as I stood in that line but we were all impeccable and the white immigration officer didn't have the slightest idea about what was going on. You think I'm making this up but I was right in the middle of it.

blithely

billowing
azure & crimson paper carp
tethered
to a sky-high pole

tassels

this roundabout
saunter
thru Gotenyama backstreets
re sound-
ing inside the shell
of a child's
syntax

(an 'echo'
of a distant echo. . .

my mother
taught me on the Sunday morning
back porch
of a long ago East Calgary
circa 1930s

these
thrasht blossoms clinging to my sleeve

       this mid-morning
       reprieve

from *Gotenyama* (1985)

Part Three

All Caught Up in Our Canadian Lives

hen I arrived in Victoria I didn't know any English. Papa on the other hand had been in Canada for ten years so he spoke and wrote English well. Needless to say he didn't have the time or patience to teach me so I pricked up my ears and bit by bit picked it up by myself. It's all so confusing because the sounds I make never match the way the words look on the printed page. You could say I've never learned English properly but I have learned how to take care of myself. My friends say Mary you have a way of speaking your mind forthrightly and that's what really matters.

Whenever the big ocean liners docked in Victoria I would drop whatever I was doing and run down the street to the waterfront to gawk at all the newly arrived immigrants. You can't imagine how my ears perked up at the sound of all that familiar banter. Every summer one of the liners would stay in port to be outfitted and all the locals would be invited on board for a tour and a cup of tea. When I sipped the green tea and nibbled on a seaweed biscuit I really felt homesick.

Papa said I cried a lot at first. He said he couldn't do much to console me so he gave me a child and said you'll get over it. We had promised my father we would return in three years' time but the promise didn't comfort me because I never had any idea how long three years would be in a foreign country. Papa for his part had no desire to go back. He said there was nothing left for him in Tosa that he didn't carry around in his head.

When I arrived in Victoria a Mrs. Shimizu who had come over many years before as a picture-bride took me shopping. She was the one who helped me choose my first western clothes. I got a black suit with a long skirt, a matching hat and my first pair of leather shoes. They sure looked stylish but it took a while to learn to walk in them. Just for fun I tried on a laced corset but it couldn't do anything for my figure. The funniest part of all was putting layers of newspapers on my breasts to puff them up because all the stylish western clothes were tailored for women with big breasts. I even tried on a pair of wool panties because Mrs. Shimizu told me everybody wore them in Canada because it got so cold. O I owe Mrs. Shimizu a lot — she really did ease my way into Canadian life.

A little while ago I went to Victoria with one of my grand-daughters. It was an occasion to pay my last respects to a friend I hadn't seen since we were both living in Moose Jaw. And yes, I wanted to see if any of the old haunts were still there. With my broken English I couldn't tell my grand-daughter much about my early years there so I kept it to myself as both of us walked along. Some things hadn't changed — the old Empress Hotel still stood there in its Victorian glory. It was the biggest building I had ever seen in my life.

Now in those long ago days Papa was working in a club as a valet and waiter. The building the club occupied was right next to the Empress. It's some kind of a shop now I thought as we walked by. Our house was just down the block and around the corner, the harbour just minutes away.

Although I barely spoke any English I got a job minding the child of a wealthy American couple who owned a big shoe store. They trusted me with their child and so I taught it all the Japanese lullabies of my childhood and together we learned to speak English.

While Papa was working at the club he learned how to press suits and make them look spiffy. We were just scraping by so he made the front of our house into a dry-cleaning shop.

We had to leave the front door open it got so steamy. I took charge of the mending and sewing. Then George was born. We slept in a small room at the back of the house. I nursed George, cooked and slept when I couldn't stand on my feet. On top of that I was pregnant again.

O I wanted to tell my granddaughter I didn't have any idea what I was letting myself in for when I was her age. And even though I couldn't put words to all that went on in my head and she was speechless because it was all new we had a good time. Those streets I once knew so well made my feet sore and my ankles wobbly. The only places I remember have no fixed address but are clearly visible in my mind.

Most of us who came to Canada around Taishou 5 or 6 [1916–17] had a hard time, a very hard time. Some of the women got pledged to complete strangers and nobody told them anything about birth control so they often had more kids than they ever wanted or could afford. And if their husbands turned out to be good-for-nothing types they stuck it out because they didn't have any choice. Remember there wasn't any welfare in those days and jobs were scarce. Besides, when a Meiji man and woman got married it was for keeps.

After I'd been in Victoria for a while I got a letter from my father saying, no matter how poor we be don't send me any money, particularly Shigekiyo's hard-earned money. Ah my poor father was a man with too much pride. He thought that Papa was doing well by then. Ha! I couldn't have sent him a nickel even if I'd wanted to and there was no way I could tell him we were just scraping by. Work was scarce, wages scant, but we were young and agile. We got by in the Englishman's world. Imagine a samurai's daughter learning how to live with a hard-drinking man in a world that didn't speak Japanese. Imagine a samurai's daughter rolling up her sleeves and learning how to do mundane things for the first time.

Father wrote me regularly. He had a beautiful hand. I still have his letters in my trunk. Mariko has often said, Mom, take those old letters from your trunk and burn them. There's no point in keeping them here in Canada where nobody can read them. I tell her it's none of her business, I'll do something with them before I die. Then I tie them up into a bundle and put them back in my old steamer trunk. It's a shame that my kids didn't learn to read and write Japanese. George and Mariko can but they don't want to be reminded of their Tosa years. Let bygones be bygones, Mom. Tomorrow is what we live for.

My brother kept me informed about family matters. At first Mizuho wrote in English thinking that I must have learned English by now. When he found out that I hadn't he wrote in Japanese. He was poor as a temple mouse. I once sent him the five yen I kept in my trunk. It was only five yen but he wrote thanking me as if it were five hundred yen. I've had to be frugal all my life but money never meant that much to me. I've always known it couldn't buy happiness. I've known embittered Issei who only saw their lives through the hardships they endured. And I've known others who simply trusted that their small deeds might shine in the everyday world. It's taken me a long lifetime to see things straight.

Papa, baby George and I didn't catch the German flu though lots of people we knew came down with it and some of them died. Luckily one of Papa's buddies came by with a big bottle of whisky. Papa always swore it was that scotch that saved the three of us. He even put a teaspoonful in George's milk bottle. We heard they called it German flu because it was brought home by the troops who had fought the Germans on the western front. It was awful. Those we knew who came down with it got a high fever and their faces turned purple. Ask anybody who lived in Victoria back then how awful that flu was.

Then [in 1920] my father wrote saying he was ill and wanted to see us and would we come home as we had promised. Papa didn't want to go. He had long ago given up the notion of becoming Father's heir so he borrowed the money for my boat-fare from the manager of the club, plus fifty dollars for spending money, and put George and me on the boat. I was pregnant with Mariko who was born in Kochi. For two years I played the part of the dutiful daughter and a full-time moth-er and I enjoyed every moment of it.

O I remember Manzou Nagano. He was on the boat when I went back to Japan. Nagano-san was one of our Victoria neighbours. We used to visit back and forth. He said good-bye to George and me in Kobe and went on his way and that was the last time I saw him. I was sure surprised to read in the *JCCA Bulletin* that Nagano-san was the first Japanese to come to Canada. I didn't know this. I don't think he did either. We were just a couple of Issei on our way home for a visit. That was seventy years ago. Nagano-san would be surprised to know that I'm still alive and kicking.

When I took George back to Umagi my father-in-law looked me up and down and said, my but haven't we got a haughty bride on our hands. I asked him what he meant and he said, you seem to have forgotten how to bow properly.

I looked him in the eye and said people in Canada don't bow to each other, they shake hands instead. He wasn't impressed and there was no way I could convince him that a person picked up new customs in a foreign land. After all he had never left Shikoku. It was long after the war when TV came to Umagi and he saw his first white man. As far as he was concerned they were the infidels who had ushered in the Meiji era.

That first time when I returned to Umagi with George a part of me didn't want to be there but I had to show them their first grandson. I didn't care for the damp mountain air and there was nobody for me to visit. The days passed. The Kiyookas could see that I was glum. You'll be happier under your parents' roof for the rest of your stay, they said, and put me on the bus into town. Boy was I glad to leave. If I had had to spent my life in Umagi I sure wouldn't have married Papa. O it's easy to say my fate was sealed when I married him but if you're just twenty you're ready for new adventure.

When I first got back to Kochi, Father eyed me intently and without hesitation said that I had become a creature he barely recognized and he didn't like what he beheld. I told him I didn't feel that way but if I was different it couldn't be helped because I was mixing with all kinds of people who only spoke English — weeks went by and the only Japanese I heard I heard whispering inside my own head. I couldn't convey all this to Father but I made up for it by being the dutiful daughter again. It didn't take long to fall back into the old family routine. As I've said, Father loved his sake. He drank ichi-gou [one serving of just under quarter of a litre]. He also loved his sashimi fresh so come rain or shine . I went out and got sake and sashimi for him. There was a sake shop just down the street but Father didn't like their brew so I had to go to a sake shop a few blocks away. The fishmonger and I became friends and I found myself greeting old shopkeepers as if I had never left home. The seasons passed. George was ready to begin kindergarten, Mariko had begun to walk. A part of me didn't want to return to Canada.

Those two years I spent in Kochi are among the best years of my life. And as it turned out, it would be the last time Father and I would stroll together in our old precinct.

One night we were taking our ease in front of the hibachi when he asked me how things were going for the two of us in faraway Canada. I didn't want to say a thing about the matter but Father had asked so I told him just how hard it was.

He looked at me sternly and said, you had better give the kids up to the Kiyookas and come home. I've made a big mistake. I was shocked by his bluntness. The very idea of giving up my kids made me angry and I told him so. I said, Father I wouldn't think of giving my kids to anybody. You should know that. Besides, it's not your fault: Papa and I have only ourselves to blame. Father never mentioned it again but played the part of the doting grandfather.

While I was gone Papa heard that there was work in Moose Jaw so he decided that we should go there. After all he wasn't getting anywhere in Victoria. We agreed that it would be best if I left George and Mariko with their grandparents till we got on our feet. So one evening I asked Father if he would give Papa and me three more years and if things didn't get better I would return home. Father hadn't forgotten his stake in our future so he agreed and that was that.

I had been in Tosa for nearly two years when I reluctantly took leave of George and Mariko. There was a young girl from mother's side of the family who was living in and helping out. I often left the kids in her care while I was out visiting or buying Father's sake and sashimi. Now she was carrying Mariko on her back as I took my leave. They waved and waved and turning I waved back but I made sure they didn't see my tears. I had just taken George to Umagi to live with his grandparents, and now I was leaving Mariko in Kochi with mine. It was the promise of returning for the two of them in three years' time that kept me going. Lots of Issei families went through the same kind of separations though they don't like to talk about it because it's still too painful to recall. Papa and I worked hard but the kids kept coming and I couldn't keep the promise I'd made.

On the boat taking me back to Canada I met this nice-looking guy from Osaka who was on his way to California. He asked me where I was going. I told him I'm on my way to a small prairie town I can't even name on the other side of the Rockies. He said I'd better watch out because my passport could be confiscated and I could find myself taken into custody, even sold into prostitution.

O no, that won't happen to me. I have a husband waiting for me at the other end, I said, as if saying so could hide my feelings. O I felt my heart beating for this brash young guy in a way I never felt for Papa. One afternoon as we sauntered around the upper deck together he stopped me in midstride and said, let's you and I go off to California together.

I reminded him that I already had a husband and that one man at a time was all I could handle. There was no doubt in my mind that we found each other attractive but that was it. O there were other men who were fond of me and asked for my hand but none of them equalled this three-week boat romance.

You know, when a Meiji man and woman got married it was for keeps. In my grandparents' time a samurai's daughter would be given a nuptial sword as part of her dowry and she'd be told in no uncertain terms once you leave home you belong to your husband's family. If you have to leave his household use the sword.

My Kyoto aunt was given a nuptial sword which she said she promptly put away and forgot about. Well one afternoon she took it out of the dark closet and wiping the dust off its lacquered sheath she handed it over to me saying, the first time I held it was when it was given to me. The second time was when I put it away in the closet. And now the third and last time is this moment I hand it over to you. I bowed and took it from her and slowly withdrew the shining blade. Thumbing its keen edge I thought of all the times in my life I might have reached for it. Slipping it back into its sheath I thanked her for the gift. When I got back to Canada I passed it on to my son Harry who likes to collect things Japanese.

When I got back to Victoria Papa had already packed up all our belongings and before I knew it we were boarding the CPR train in Vancouver. It was our first sight of the mountains. Boy we were impressed. On our way we decided to stop off in Banff. We ended up staying three months. Papa got a job as a bellhop, I worked as a chambermaid. You could say we had a holiday but the truth was we didn't have enough money to pay the first month's rent in Moose Jaw.

O I'll never forget that trip through the Rockies and that slow trip across the limitless prairies. Papa and I had never seen anything like it. We Issei came from one small prefecture or another we knew the boundaries of. Boy, was I dismayed by the distances between people, places and things in Canada.

But that didn't stop us. Like other immigrants, we really
wanted to succeed.

Mr. Kuwabara is a good example. He never got to high school
but he had lots of energy and made a big fortune growing
mushrooms. Mr. Mimori was among the first Issei to get into
gardening and he's well known for his gardening. Papa and I
never had anything but the lowest paying jobs, but we did
have the freedom to move all over the place which we could-
n't have done if we had remained in Nippon.

I don't really know how Papa got a job in the Royal Hotel
in Moose Jaw but I do know I ended up working there as
a chambermaid. In the twenties there was just a handful of
Issei families and a number of single guys in Moose Jaw.
The times were good if you weren't at the bottom of the
social ladder. Only the guys who had learned a family trade
and knew how to use their skills over here succeeded.
All the unskilled guys like Papa never earned more than
a basic wage and each job lasted as long as there was a
prosperity.

We knew a single guy from Ehime-ken who worked all day
on the railroad but had lodgings downtown. And we knew
this couple from Akita. He worked in the same hotel as we
did and had a really good-looking wife. She was a proud one
with her thick black hair and everybody knew she was far
too nice to other men. She wasn't exactly a prostitute, but
thanks to her husband who put her on a pedestal she had
lots of time on her hands and not enough money to live the

way she felt she deserved to. So there were all these single guys around who dreamt of taking her in their arms and this guy was one of them. Anyhow he fell by one afternoon on a casual visit and after that he couldn't stay away.

He spent all his hard-earned money buying her favours. One day he implored her to run away with him but she told him bluntly that she would never think of leaving her husband who was a very jealous man. So he decided to leave town but not before he had made love to her one last time. She for her part had already used him up and told him to go away when he arrived at her door. Furious, he pushed his way into the house and chased her around the living room, then ran into the kitchen and grabbed up a big kitchen knife and stabbed her several times.

Now the couple who ran the small store at the front of the house told me they were minding their business when they heard all the screaming. They went around to the back to see what was going on and found her all hacked up in a pool of blood.

As for him he walked over to the police station and told them in his broken English that he had just wanted to make love to her and had no intention of harming her till she made him feel like an asshole. Then he lost his mind and what happened happened without him. Her husband returned to Nippon with his wife's ashes. Years later we heard that he died of TB but I'm pretty sure he died of a broken heart.

In those days there were lots of Issei men who never had a woman to sleep with. For most of them there wasn't much to do after a hard day's work besides drinking, gambling and going to the prostitute. Most of them lived like monks in dingy housekeeping rooms and as often as not slowly drank themselves to death. Some had unwanted kids. Others got syphillis, TB and clap. A small handful overcame the odds and succeeded in a modest way. And of course there were Issei women who made a living by sleeping around. Most of them had husbands who knew what was going on but simply put up with it. After all it didn't matter where the money came from when the going was tough.

It's no wonder that young women of my generation got cheated into prostitution. If you were from a poor inaka [country bumpkin] family and some guy came along and waved a handful of yen in front of your parents' nose the chances were good you'd be sold. And guess who raked in all the money at this end? Folks like Mr. and Mrs. So and So who had a thriving prostitution house in the Interior. I knew them and others.

Most Issei don't want to talk about it but I know that it happened all over the West and it happened because most Issei men didn't have a wife, never mind a girlfriend. They didn't have a woman because Japanese women who weren't married weren't allowed to immigrate. Some of these women lived in the neighbourhood. For them it was just a bread and butter business. Like the rest of us they had to pay for their room and board.

I know about them because I was a good friend of a former prostitute. She told me how she'd been tricked into coming to the States to work as a maid in a rich man's house and how that house turned out to be a prostitution and gambling casino. She said there was no turning back so she had to prostitute herself. She put up with all the burly white guys until she saved enough money to take her away. She wanted to earn her keep in a respectable way but try as she might she couldn't find any housework so she returned to prostitution and in the end she became the madam of her own house. She used to go to the pool hall and take on one of the locals and whip his pants off.

In her old age a white guy, a lumberjack in B.C. who had slept with her in his youth, came to visit her. They soon found out they were fond of each other and decided to spend their last years together. So in no time at all she got married. Everyone noted how she got younger and had her hair dyed red.

We knew an Issei guy in Moose Jaw who fell head over heels in love with a real redhead, the waitress where he took his meals. It was outrageous in those days because both whites and Asians frowned on mixed marriages. Well one way or another the two of them stuck it out and raised a son. When the son grew up he took his mother's English name. Lots of immigrant people changed their real names to cover up their origins. But let me tell you it was a big blow to a Meiji man. His wife is still alive and lives in an old age home in Victoria. We don't see each other often but when we do we remember our days in Moose Jaw fondly.

Roy was born there in the winter of '26 during a January blizzard. When he was six months old I got a costly telegram from my brother imploring me to hurry home because Father was gravely ill. He didn't know it but it took a month to get to Tosa. I'd have left the next morning but we were just scraping by and we hadn't been in town long enough to borrow money. I couldn't even send any condolence money.

So it was that Father passed away without seeing me. O I hope he understood how much he meant to me — I couldn't have survived without his example.

Roy's birth and Father's dying mark the end of the Taisho period and the beginnings of the Showa. The Great Depression and the Sino-Japanese war lay ahead but we Issei were all caught up in our Canadian lives.

this line hops skips & jumps along —
syllable by syllable it keeps falling back into a thronging:
all   all of your voices audible   all
breathing in the silent interstices between each letter . . .
each their own share of All Things:
"no wisdom without laughter"   the myriad kinds thereof:
itself a tongue-tide language . mythos/mirth
the girth of the whole rotund earth its ineluctable preamble .
"laugh and the world laughs with you
cry and you cry alone" — a page from the Reader's Digest
that hung on the narrow entrance wall just
above the overstuffed chair in the post-war living room .
i have always associated that homely motto
with father who had a quick laugh but seldom used it .

true charity as i know it began in my childhood home

from *October Terrain* (1985)

Pictures from the Old
Family Album

Sublime Photograph

91

This picture was taken in Opal Alberta during the forties. In those days George was just a goodlooking young guy dying to get away from home. Roy would be going on sixteen. He's the tallest in the photo and as you can see he's short-sighted. The look on Harry's face is familiar — I've seen it many times. Harry's two years younger than Roy but he's already his own guy. And there's Franky. That smile on his face is his, he still smiles that way and you can't help feeling he's a great guy. O it doesn't matter much if the boys look scruffy — at least Joyce and Irene are well-dressed. Like Franky Joyce always had a great smile. Irene could look glum even when she wasn't. In a few years they would leave home and it would be a good many years before we all got together again.

Looking through the album I'm reminded of Mariko's absence and all the pain her prolonged absence caused. Down through the years Papa and I sent her the family news as well as money and photos of her brothers and sisters. She in turn sent us an occasional note with a photo of herself and as she grew up her photos reflected an unspoken sadness. I knew long ago I would have to bear the burden of it. But I've told her many times since she joined us that it wasn't just my fault. First we had the Depression. Then in '39 the Germans invaded Czechoslovakia and ignited the Second World War. Then after Pearl Harbour we were uprooted fingerprinted and duly registered as "enemy aliens." All these horrible events overtook us and got in the way of Papa and I uniting the family. Now it turns out that Mariko's the only one I can talk with in "Kochi-ben" about our uncommonly common past.

⌐ ⌐ ⌐

This photo of George and Mariko must have been taken just before — or was it after? — I returned to Canada. George is four, Mariko two. I didn't know then that it would be many years before I saw them again. Meanwhile the kids kept coming one after the other till there were five of them. Papa and I found ourselves inside a circle of unruly kids who didn't know their big brother or sister except by photos like this. You can tell what I mean if you look intently at the photo — the way both of them are dressed tells you just how Japanese both of them grew up to be.

⌐ ⌐ ⌐

This is Papa's Mom, Yasu, and his Dad, Genichi, plus Papa's younger sister, Toshiko. And that's little George beside her. I don't know who took the photo but all four of them sure have their eyes on the camera. I wonder why Yasu's hands are hidden? Maybe it's because they were inaka [country bumpkin] hands? Or was it a portrait convention that women had to keep their hands out of sight? Hmm, I wonder if the guy who took the photo could see how it made her look like a bird with amputated wings and a pair of white tabi on her feet. This photo must have been taken soon after I left George with his grandparents. My, doesn't he look like a typical backcountry kid? Every time I look at this photo I'm reminded of my first years in Victoria and how I missed my first-born. Motherhood and grief have gone together from the beginning of my life in Canada.

⌐ ⌐ ⌐

This is one of the whaling factory photos taken in North Harbour on the Queen Charlottes. Papa and I were there [c. 1917, 1918] and we knew all these guys standing on top of the whale. The only white guy in the photo is the factory foreman. His wife was the camp cook. There weren't many women around so we became fast friends. I helped out in the kitchen. All of us Issei lived in tarpaper shacks beside the ocean and despite the brine-wind the shacks always smelled of sweaty clothes and whale blubber. From our stoop we could see the blue whales cavorting in the sea and every so often we spotted a Japanese or a Russian trawler. And all summer long the harpoon boats went out to sea to fetch themselves a whale. When they got close enough to harpoon the unsuspecting whale all the men would hang on for dear life while they rode its tail far out to sea. Then when its big heart stopped and the harpoon line went slack they towed it back to the whaling factory where it got winched up to the cutting floor so these guys could slice it up with long flaying knives. Other guys rendered the thick slabs of blubber in boiling vats. We were all Japanese so we didn't mind the daily diet of whale meat. I had had whale meat in my youth and I remember singing a song about brother whale. It was hard work but we were all young and full of ourselves.

Ah I remember this guy — Uncle Kosaka. He and his wife were graduates of the Teachers College in Kagoshima. When he got drunk he'd joke about how their education had paved the way for him to sweat it out in a blubber factory. O he had a wicked sense of humour. I wonder what happened to all the guys and I wonder if any of them are alive and kicking. Isn't it amazing! I was there seventy years ago and here I am holding this faded photo of all of us in a whaling factory.

⌐ ⌐ ⌐

This is the half-log house that Roy and Papa built on our farm in Opal. The bottom part was built of logs taken from an old log granary. Using a how-to-do-it manual and simple tools they built the half-walls, pitched roof and the small entranceway. We didn't have electricity or a bathroom and the well-water was a hundred feet away. Boy it sure got crowded at times and yes our tempers flared. But there were all those cozy winter nights around the kerosene lamp with the smell of burning wood and rising bread when it was forty below and blowing snow outside.

Before Papa passed away in the early seventies Roy drove Papa and me out to Opal one summer afternoon to have one last look around. We left the car on the side of the dirt road and walked into the old farmyard. Of course we didn't know who owned it now but we hoped they wouldn't mind. In the forties you could see the three tall grain elevators holding the sky up from the farmyard but now there wasn't a single one left standing. Our house had crumpled into a heap of rotten logs and splintered wood overgrown with thistles and weeds. The well that had been dug by hand had caved in and all that was left of the old log barn had toppled in on itself. Otherwise the land itself had the same parched look. Driving along the dirt road that was Opal's main street we tried to locate Hawreluik's General Store, the Blacksmith Shop and where the Pool Hall stood. And as we drove out of Opal we agreed that Opal had become for us just another "ghost town," one of many we had thrived in.

⌐ ⌐ ⌐

This is the clapboard house we lived in during the thirties. It stood on the corner of Third Street East and Tenth Avenue across from the Parkhill Bedding Company. Now all along Tenth the tall red CPR fence demarcated the Freight Sheds, the Ice House, and miles of tracks from the houses running all the way to First Street West. From our second floor bathroom window we could always tell the time of day from the tall clock tower on top of City Hall. To the left of Roy's bike all the way to the corner of Tenth Avenue Papa and I had a large garden that we looked after every summer. This is the clapboard house in east Calgary all the kids grew up in.

O I could go on and on about this house and all the people who passed through it. One of the bright ones was Hayakawa-san who was on his way to Chicago to complete his studies. Papa and I put up with having single Issei guys living with us because we needed the money. On weekends all sorts of single guys came by to drink and play poker. Things were lean but you wouldn't have known it if you had dropped by on a Sunday afternoon with all the kids underfoot and all the guys getting drunk and talking their fool heads off.

Boy if Roy's CCM bike wasn't there in this photo you'd swear the house was abandoned. I mean there's not a single child in sight. Who is it who goes on living in the house of memory but a once-immigrant mother?

⌐ ⌐ ⌐

This one was taken some time after George joined us. You can see that he's almost as tall as me and a lot older than Roy and Harry. Look, all the guys have got neckties on and they've all got tweed caps on their heads or in their hands. Tweed caps were popular if you wanted to look real spiffy. And isn't it odd how large Roy and Harry's caps look in their small hands? Roy's just started wearing long pants. Harry's still in shorts. If you look between them you'll see that I'm wearing white hose and elegant shoes tied with a black bow. Boy! none of the kids look happy. They must have been taken away from their play and resented being dressed up. Anyhow Papa and I wanted a new portrait of the family with George in it to send to George's grandparents. We thought a recent family photo would reassure them that their George was where he belonged.

This was taken in front of our house in Calgary. Roy was growing fast. See he's a whole head taller than Harry and he's already short-sighted. O I didn't notice before but Harry's sticking his tongue out. He's on his way to being a rascal. I don't know why both of them wore glasses so young. Papa never wore glasses in his life and I didn't until old age. I like that smirk on Joyce's face and the way she's holding onto Franky's hand. Franky was meant to be the last — until Irene came along. And isn't it funny that all the guys are wearing their Maple Leaf hockey sweaters? My, how Canadian can an immigrant family get!

⌐ ⌐ ⌐

My father had a samurai's passion for swordsmanship and poetry. He had a fine voice and loved to sing his favourite poems. Some of the bright students from the local high school used to come by to study poetry with him. One of them found me attractive and started writing love letters. I wasn't too sure how to respond but I was flattered. Well one night long after I had said goodnight Father caught me reading the love letters. He was furious. He snatched them from me and to my dismay ripped them up into little pieces. Next day he went to the boy's home to scold his parents for their son's impudence. Father could sure be gruff.

And then the only son of a samurai family who lived nearby took a fancy to me and began writing me florid love letters.

Well one night while I was reading them Father leaned over my shoulder and read along with me. After we finished he said, My, this lad is so full of himself he doesn't see the shape of his true feelings. I was lucky I didn't fall for him because he died of pneumonia after graduating from high school. O there were several others but none of them turned out to be as bright and venturesome as Papa.

You see if a Meiji woman was caught exchanging love letters let alone sidelong glances she was certain to be reprimanded. What's called "the dating game" here didn't exist in my Kochi. We were not encouraged to seek out male friends. Most of my generation's marriages were prearranged. Things were kind of strict I guess but I must say it didn't feel that way. I mean that's just the way it was. An old proverb says the bride who is lucky enough to be wedded to a kind man will find love in due time. Love wasn't a big issue as long as kindness and family piety prevailed.

⌐ ⌐ ⌐

This picture was taken as I boarded the train in Victoria. See how round my face is. I'm twenty-five. O look at my hat! Women like me who couldn't afford the latest fashion always made their own hats. You went out and bought the pattern and the right amount of material and all the other stuff and you laid the cloth out on the table and pinned the paper pattern to the cloth. Then you cut out each part and you pinned all the parts together and stitched till it looked like the very hat on the model's head on the pattern-book cover. See the overcoat I'm wearing? Well it's back in fashion. I saw one just like it the other day in a very fashionable ladies' store. Even when I couldn't afford it I always wanted to be well-dressed. It has something to do with feeling good about yourself.

⌐ ⌐ ⌐

This is Mr. Kanou from Tosa who worked as the desk-man in a big Saskatoon hotel. Now everybody who knew him said that he was bright enough to be the hotel manager one day. Well one night while Kano-san was tipping the bottle and smoking in bed he dozed off. Before he knew what was happening his bed had caught on fire and the room turned into a blazing tinder box. By the time the firemen arrived to put out the blaze Kano-san was burned to a crisp. This awful fire happened in the early hours on Easter Sunday. A mutual friend in Saskatoon phoned to tell us what had happened.

This other guy came from Kochi City. I've forgotten his name but he was one of the top graduates of Okayama High School and he became a much respected doctor. These two guys and Papa were real buddies. The three of them excelled in the martial arts and whenever they got together they would toast their bright Meiji futures.

O look! there's something on the back. It says "Shogatsu, Pine and Moon: Sugatsu, Autumn Moon: Jugatsu, Full Moon in Mirror: Meiji '39." Hmmm I wonder if this has something to do with their horoscopes. You know Japanese guys often formed their deepest bonds during high school and the friendships would last a lifetime but poor Papa lost all his friends when he immigrated to Canada.

⌐ ⌐ ⌐

This one was taken by Mr. Iwama on New Year's Day. Roy, who has his hands around a beer bottle, is just a kid so it must have been taken around 1930. O I can't remember the names of the kids beside him but that's Patsy Iwama in her kimono leaning on Mr. Ishida's arm. Patsy came along years after her brothers had grown up. Mr. Ishida was the eldest son and black sheep of a respectable Kyoto family. With a twinkle in his eye he would tell you that he was born under the eaves of Sanjusangendo [a famous pagoda].

The plump woman in the floral dress behind him is Mrs. Iwama. She loved having her friends in for afternoon tea and indulging in the local gossip. After Pearl Harbour she took Patsy and her brother Freddy back to Nippon and that's the last we saw of her.

That's pretty Mrs. Matsuoka beside her who up and died of TB before she even had a child. Next to her is pop-eyed me. I've had my hair curled. I didn't know then that I would have four more kids. Next is Mrs. Iwama's sister. She also went back and the last thing I heard was that she was living by herself in Osaka.

The woman beside her is from Kagoshima. We all knew she made extra money seducing all sorts of men in the back room of her barber shop but we didn't make a big deal out of it. I mean things were really hard and everybody did what they had to to survive. You can sure tell that the guy beside her is a bit of a dandy. And the guy in the pin-striped suit sitting behind Roy was one of the frugal ones who saved every cent and returned to his own prefecture to live the life of a squire.

And that's Frank Iwama the number two son standing behind his mother and beside him is George Matsuoka who was Papa's drinking buddy. Poor George. He thought it was the end of the world when his beautiful young wife up and died. We thought George was going to drink himself to death and take Papa with him but George pulled himself together. He returned to Nippon to fetch himself a new wife.

Lastly there's Roy Iwama. Shortly after this photo was taken he left Calgary for Eastern Canada and nobody has ever heard from him since. Fred their number three son isn't present because he went back to Nippon with his mother. Papa isn't in the picture. He never cared much for parties and had the added excuse that he had to be on duty that afternoon.

Mr. Iwama worked for many years as a porter at the Palliser Hotel. Quite unexpectedly he up and died one day of acute pneumonia. All his friends said it was the noxious darkroom chemicals that perforated his lungs. O this photo of a long-ago New Year's party wouldn't be in my hands without Mr. Iwama's avid eye. And it's comforting to know that we're all presided over by a tableau of Shinto gods and goddesses attired in their regalia. Household deities who share a niche in one's livingroom are the only useful gods. The other gods are too far away to be really useful.

This photo of my father is the one that hung in the living room of all the houses we lived in. The one I keep on my night table now. It's the last photo Father had taken on the cusp of the Showa era. It was enlarged and printed by Mr. Iwama.

Kane Oe (Mary's Mother)

Mizuho Oe (Mary's only brother
and his son Hiroshi)

for Mariko
and Mariko

the sash you bought of my ukata
is firm around my waist

each time i tie it   you
are on one end & i am on the other

how else tell of a brother & sister,
thirty years parted, drawn,

together, again

from *Kyoto Airs* (1964)

Part Four

Keeping the Dream of Uniting the Family Alive

hen the Royal Hotel closed its doors at the beginning of the Depression Papa and I lost our jobs. And so we said goodbye to the few friends we had in Moose Jaw and boarded the CPR train to take us to Calgary. Harry and Joyce and the others were all born there.

In Calgary there were more Japanese families and single guys. Boy, some of them like Furusako-san the barber were real characters. He was one of your old-fashioned single guys who lived in a simple room in a large boarding house. And as far as we could tell he never had anything to do with women. He was a middle-aged guy who always wore a green eye-shade and listened to everybody's small talk while making them look spiffy. And of course he saved every penny. When the war came to its bitter end, Furusako-san sold his barber shop and returned to Yamaguchi prefecture as he had all along planned. We got a letter from him in later years in which he wondered if his whole life had been nothing but a barber shop dream.

Then there was my friend Mrs. Watanabe who told me how she left home at sixteen. She went to Brazil with hundreds of poor Japanese who signed contracts to work on the big coffee and sugar plantations. She said they all lived in hovels and worked all day long in the sweltering heat for nothing but a bellyful of gruel. She hated being treated like a slave so she hid herself in a sugar-cane cart with only the clothes on her back and got away. It's a long story but one way or another she made it up to Seattle where her older sister worked as a prostitute. They had a hard time making ends meet so they decided to move to Calgary and there despite themselves they ended up working in the Chinese prostitution house. There she met this Japanese guy who was a graduate of Waseda University and a bit of a dandy. He talked her into marrying him. Just before Pearl Harbour the two of them took their savings and moved to Opal Alberta. It was thanks to them that we got through the war.

There were lots of women in those days who got tricked into prostitution by agents who gave them a handful of change, an address at the end and put them on the boat. Now most of these young women came from poor prefectures in northern Japan like Amori and Fukushima. It's awful to say but their parents were in such dire need during a long famine they sold their daughters into prostitution. It still goes on all over Asia. Too many children and too little to eat turns young women into a commodity.

I knew a Hiroshima woman who became a prostitute that way. She got herself pregnant and gave birth to an albino child. She had slept with so many men she had no idea who the child's father was. In those days people looked down on albino children not to mention their mother so she took the child and went to the States where she met a Black guy who fell madly in love with her. They had several kids and though things weren't easy for a mixed couple her life improved. I knew her in her old age and admired her. She had survived all the scars of her profession without loss of pride while the city she grew up in and never returned to lay in ashes.

In the thirties there was a prostitution house in the heart of Chinatown that mostly catered to lonely Chinese guys and other Asians. Most of the women were cheated. They were told they could make lots of money and then when they came they couldn't go back even if they wanted to. They felt so ashamed and they had nowhere to go, no choice but to die there. One of the Japanese prostitutes who worked there was a real beauty but she got infected with a strange disease that deformed her body. In the end she just couldn't bear the sight of herself so to put an end to all her misery she torched the house. Wherever you find single men and penurious women you can be sure that someone will start up a brothel. It's always been that way. Calgary wasn't any different.

Recently at a big Issei celebration I noticed this white-haired guy looking over at me as if he knew me but I couldn't place him. After all the speeches and the big dinner he came up to me and said, Remember me? I'm Tomimoto. I owe you my life when I was down and out. I'm glad we've met — at last I can say thank you.

Well as soon as I heard that funny drawl I remembered him. He was one of the single guys who had stayed with us awhile at 1008 Third Street East. He used to get his hair cut at Furusako-san's barber shop. It was sixty years or more since we first met but there we were talking it up like it was yesterday.

Ah but those years swept through us like the prairie wind scattering everything before it. We had far too many kids and far too little money. Papa and I had promised Father we would return in three years' time to take up our family duties. That's why Father gave us his whole-hearted blessing. He really wanted to believe he had made the right choice on my behalf and that Papa would one day replace him as the Iai master. But things just didn't work out. I know Papa felt badly about that broken promise even though he had long ago made up his mind to become a Canadian.

I had taken George to Umagi when he was three and left him there with his grandparents. Mariko was with my parents until she was six when my father took her to Umagi to live with her other grandparents. George and Mariko knew they had brothers and sisters because we wrote to them regularly and sent along the latest snapshots.

Ah it's too bad but those ten years George spent in Umagi have turned out to be the very heart of our estrangement. From the very day George came to join us Papa and I had a hard time understanding him. George is seventy-plus now but I still feel a coolness when I'm in his company. I know he can't help it and I can't do a thing to warm him up. We don't share a sense of humour and he hasn't any memory of how proud I was of my first-born son and all the hours we spent together in a long-ago Victoria.

It was different with the other kids who came one after the other during the late twenties and thirties. They grew up under one roof in East Calgary and if there was a squabble between them they had to make up because they sat beside each other at meals and slept paired in the same bed. More importantly they grew up inside the whiteman's world. George and Mariko didn't have that bond. They were tied to their grandparents. Papa and I wrote to them regularly. If we had a few yen to spare we sent that on. It was the least we could do. Papa and I had a hard time keeping the dream of uniting the family alive. Many Issei families were separated for years. It's too painful to talk about all these bereftments so we Issei have kept them to ourselves.

Mariko used to complain that her brothers and sisters never call her "oneisan" [elder sister]. She thought it was rude to call someone by their given name like Canadians do. I guess she's very Japanese that way. Whenever she speaks of George she refers to him as "onisan" [elder brother] because that's how she related to him in Tosa.

Mariko and I live together. We seldom talk much about those disparate years but when we do all her bitterness comes out and she looks at me as if I were a stranger. She has said many times that Papa and I abandoned her when she was a child. O it's true Mariko grew up without the company of her brothers and sisters but I tell her Papa and I never meant to abandon her. I remind her once again that the Depression and the Second World War had a lot to do with it. It wasn't at all personal. But she wants to burden me with all her displacement.

George was a thirteen-year old Japanese kid when Papa brought him back to Canada [1931]. He was wearing a kasuri-cloth [traditional cotton cloth] kimono and his favourite school cap. Now I don't know what happened to that school cap but I've kept the kimono in my trunk all these years. One day when George came by I got the kimono out and showed it to him. You wore this on your back when you arrived in Canada. Why don't you take it and show it to your kids? I'm sure they'd be curious.

Without taking it from my hands George stared at it and said it wouldn't mean anything to them. Well if that's how you feel I'll put it away. And that was the end of his kasuri cloth kimono's luckless wait. What mothers remember in time is usually forgotten. That's why I'm talking this way. Big steamer trunks with strong brass clasps don't mean much these days when everyone flies, but let me tell you, for an Issei big steamer trunks hold the heart's journeyings. All that I value is locked up in that trunk.

Papa could get mad when the kids went against his wishes. I remember him smacking George because George had stayed out long after he was told to be home. George ran out of the house hollering that he was never coming back. I thought Papa had gone too far. After all George had only recently become a part of the family. Anyhow we looked all over for him and we found him curled up in the basement coal-bin. He cried I WANT TO GO BACK TO UMAGI all night long. I couldn't stand it and I couldn't console him. It was too late for Papa to act the part of a stern father and I the doting mother.

Papa and I didn't get into arguments very often because he wasn't the kind of guy to indulge in small-talk. I mean despite a large family and many friends Papa remained the solitary type. He loved nothing better than a good book and a shot of whisky. Sometimes when he drank too much he would complain about my indulgences and all the ways I spoiled the kids. I learned the hard way not to argue with a drunkard. When Papa read my silences he picked up his book as if nothing untoward had happened. Believe me that's how we spent our days in each other's company. It wasn't much fun. We seldom went anywhere together. Really, I don't know the kind of woman who could have made Papa lively — it wasn't me. You could say we were a typical Meiji couple who learned the hard way how to survive in Canada while enduring each other's foibles.

Our kids could see how hard Papa and I had to work to keep the family clothed and fed and I'm sure that told them they would have to work hard for their own livelihood. One summer afternoon I overheard our neighbour talking to Papa over the back fence. You've got lots of mouths to feed and you're just getting by, he said, so why don't you send your kids out to work? Papa liked this guy. Hell, Larry, you could be right but the way I see it there's no real hurry. Once they get a good education they'll be able to take care of Mom and me though we're not counting on it. I didn't catch Larry's answer. I was behind a hedge picking snow peas.

Papa and I haven't had anything of value to leave them. All we could do was be there for them if and when they needed us. And like I've said, Papa came over to study western ways but things didn't work out for him. He wanted his kids to be educated so they could claim the freedom he felt he never had.

All during the thirties Papa and I ran a fruit and veggie stall in the marketplace right across from the old City Hall. You could buy everything under one roof and it was just a fifteen minute walk from home. Now all the kids were growing fast and they were always hungry so we brought all the spoiled fruit and veggies home and ate them. O I loved the hubbub of the marketplace especially on Saturdays when all the country people came to town. We made more money on Saturdays than the whole of the rest of the week. We didn't have a cash register. We made change from a tin cigar box. Only the big stall keepers had proper cash registers. The Chinese stall owners all used an abacus to tote up the price of things. After counting every nickel and dime they put it in a bag and hung it around their necks. It was an odd sight to see them closing down their stalls with their money bags around their necks. And woe to anybody who wanted to take it away from them.

When we lived at 100 Third Street East the Johnsons lived around the corner and down the street towards the end of Tenth Avenue and Fourth Street next to the Alberta Produce. We knew Mr. Johnson had been a foot soldier in World War One. He had trouble with his lungs but he was a robust man who used to have a beer with Papa and worked as a grave-digger in the cemetery across the river behind the fair grounds.

Roy remembers biking to that cemetery with Buck who was the Johnsons' oldest son to see how his Pa was doing and to bum a dime. While Mr. Johnson threw dirt up from the bot-tom of a grave Roy and Buck turned on the cemetery hose and gleefully flushed gophers out of their holes. Then the two of them would bike off with a dime in their pockets for their afternoon treat at Switzer's soda fountain.

Mrs. Johnson was a tall lean woman who spent her days cooking and mending for her large family when she wasn't tending an even larger garden. Every time their tabby cat had another litter she would flush the unwanted kittens down the toilet without a second thought. The Johnsons had three boys and three girls including a set of twins. We had six kids by then — four boys and two girls — Mariko wasn't with us in those days. Their kids and ours often paired up and come rain or shine you could be sure they were hatching mischief somewhere. O I tell you we mothers had our hands full.

Harry, our third son, was the quiet one but he often got into scraps. It wasn't always his fault. The local bullies picked on him because they thought he was just a runt. Other times he got called "dirty" names and lost his temper. I don't know how many times he had his specs broken and his nose bloodied. I stopped counting. But he wasn't the only one who got into mischief. All the boys in the neighbourhood did. Black eyes, blue knees, bloody noses, bruised shins, nail in bare foot: all these could be counted on. Compared to the boys the girls were easy to bring up.

One hot summer afternoon I got so fed up with having a bunch of young brats hanging around the house I kicked them out. They straggled out the front door and down the steps across Third Street to disappear around the corner. They were on their way to the Massey Harris Company where they often played on the farm machinery. Now the Massey Harris had a large loading platform beside the railway tracks and on that loading platform there was a tall steel crane for lifting and moving heavy machinery. I knew that crane well because it towered above my head whenever I went down the alley to buy a loaf of bread.

That afternoon I was about to take a nap when I heard Harry holler, MOM, MY FINGER! MY FINGER! Harry had got the middle finger of his left hand caught in the gears of that huge crane while the other kids gleefully turned the iron handle that swung the crane around. He came running home with blood dripping all over his shoes. I was so shocked when I met him at the front door I didn't know what to do. Papa was at work. Fortunately a Mr. Kinoshita who was one of our boarders heard the wailing and came downstairs and took charge.

He wrapped Harry's hand up in a towel and hailed a neighbour who was passing by in his Model T and had him take the two of them to the hospital. Though Harry's fingertip was badly mangled I'd hoped the doctors would look kindly on it and stitch it together. Instead they just chopped it off like a chicken's head and sewed up the stump. It was sure awful to look at. It took Harry a long time to get over the loss of his fingertip but after the accident he began changing from a rascal into a quiet guy with an iron will.

Harry is the only lefty in our family and he was the only one who got scolded for it. His teachers used to poke fun at his slant-writing and do their best to change him into a right-hander but Harry resisted. To be a lefty in those days was worse than being knock-kneed or pigeon-toed.

Forty years later Roy lost the same fingertip. He sliced his off on a power-saw while he was making one of his cedar sculptures. I wonder what it means when two brothers lose the same fingertip.

There was another awful accident that happened in the early thirties. In those days the hot water tank with its small gas heater happened to be the warmest corner in the house. So the first kids up on a winter morning would run downstairs in their nightgowns and throw open the door of the heater to stand in front of the flames. That morning as I lay in bed wondering what the new year held for us I heard Roy shout MOM! MOM! I'M BURNING! I leapt out of bed and ran into the kitchen. Through the smoke I could see Roy's nightgown up in flames. With my bare hands and a wet towel I put the flames out but it was too late. Roy got scorched from his shoulders down to the small of his back. I'll never forget the smell of his burnt flesh.

The two of them had been pushing and shoving each other for the warm spot in front of the heater and before either of them knew what happened Roy's nightgown caught on fire. I mentioned the occasion to Harry years ago. He nodded and turned away. All he said was he's never forgotten that New Year's morning. You really couldn't blame one or the other but I know Harry has blamed himself.

Even George had an awful thing happen to him when he was a kid in Umagi. He was on his way to Kochi to spend the weekend with his city grandparents. He was looking forward to his stay as he stood at the open door of the coach peering out. Before he knew what happened his head hit a wall and it knocked him out. My brother said it was a matter of life or death but George survived. Imagine how I felt getting the news ten thousand miles away.

It's not an easy job raising kids because kids all have their own minds from the beginning. And it's funny because once they become adults they think they did it all by themselves. But I tell you mothers know who it was who put the ice pack on their head and who held their hand and prayed for them when they broke a leg.

Young couples these days have nothing but money on their minds. They want to make enough money to buy a big house in the suburbs and put their old parents in a seniors' home. Too bad. They don't understand that old people often die of loneliness. By the time they come to understand what their parents have given them and want to thank them it's often too late. If you can't stand having your parents around how do you cope when the whole world leans in on you?

My own kids don't act that way. Mariko practises the traditional devotions. She makes a regular trip to the cemetery to place fresh flowers on Papa's grave and tidy up its surroundings. George doesn't do that. I guess he still has a gripe against Papa. But now that his own kids are all grown up and have left home I think he knows what being a father means. There'll come a day when he pays Papa a visit. Roy's always lived away from the rest of us but he visits Papa whenever he comes to Edmonton. Harry and his wife Kate join us for Christmas each year and always make it a point to visit Papa's grave. Joyce and Irene fall by whenever it comes to mind. So one way or another Papa goes on having the companionship of his kids.

At Papa's last rites at the Park Memorial Chapel in '74 the minister told everyone that Papa, like so many Asian immigrants, had a harsh life but for all that he was among the fortunate ones for having had seven children who've all become exemplary Canadians. The minister said all this in front of Papa's family and friends and it's true I guess. He worked hard all his life to be a good Canadian and his last wish was to be buried in Edmonton. How a scholarly young guy from Umagi with a lively curiosity arrived in Canada at eighteen and raised seven kids only to end his days working in a garment factory is the substance of his story.

I've always had lots of friends and most of them happened to be plain white people. Papa on the other hand didn't have many friends. When we had the stall in the City Hall Market many people came to buy fruit and veggies when I was there but when Papa took over nobody dropped by but his no-account drinking cronies. Papa was a nice guy but he had too much pride to be a fruit and vegetable peddler.

Anyhow, one summer in Calgary Papa left me to run the grocery stall by myself. His father was on his death-bed so he went back to Umagi-mura for his last rites. Papa took Roy with him. Papa's relatives were all astonished that Roy could speak both Japanese and English. They themselves had never seen or heard a whiteman.

While Papa and Roy were in Umagi-mura I hired a Chinese guy we knew to help out. Business was brisk until the trouble in Manchuria hit the headlines. Then everything began to turn sour. All of our regular customers began to keep their distance. They acted like I had become the enemy. Even the Chinese market gardeners who came by in the early morning to sell us veggies cut us off. I had to depend on my Chinese help to get our daily supply. The Chinese stall-owners with whom we had been friends began pointing their fingers at me. Others kept their distance and talked about me behind my back. O I wanted to say I've been in Canada for more than twenty years and I don't have anything to do with the Japanese military presence in China, so stop it! The white stall-owners thought it was just another Oriental family quarrel.

After Papa and Roy came back from Japan I had Franky [1933]. I didn't want to take him to the market every day like I did the other kids so I told Papa I wanted to stay home. Papa said all right and carried on by himself for a while but we both knew our days in the City Hall Market were num-bered. So then he got a job in the Carlton Hotel. By the time the Japanese bombed Pearl Harbour we Issei already knew in our hearts we were in for a hard time.

Even as the first rumblings of a distant war echoed up and down the streets and back alleys of our neighbourhood we tried our best to keep our sense of humour. In those days to get extra food for his family Mr. Johnson got up early to go downtown and take his place in a long line with hundreds of destitute men. I avoided them when I went downtown to shop because the sight of so many wretched men turned my stomach. You see our house was beside the CPR tracks. From our second floor bathroom window you could see all the hobos leaping off the boxcars and running for cover before the CPR cops came after them. And because we lived on the near side of the tall CPR fence and they had kicked a hole in it to escape through, we were among the first homes they came to for a handout. Mind you we were just getting by ourselves but we couldn't turn them away so I made stacks of sandwiches and kept a thermos of coffee for them beside the front door. All those hollow-eyed men who rode the empty boxcars across the prairies during the thirties — they still haunt my vision of "O Canada."

After she had completed grade school in Umagi, her grandfather had sent Mariko off to Kyoto to live with my aunt and uncle and attend high school. My aunt and uncle had been so busy running their market they hadn't had time for sex let alone kids and by then it was too late. One day Papa suggested that they might think of adopting Mariko. After all, he said, Mariko's been living with the two of you so long she's more your daughter than my own. They said, let us think about it — it's such a grave decision on her behalf. Then they told Papa, what we need of course is a dutiful son but we will make sure Mariko gets a good education by the time you return to fetch her.

In 1938 my Kyoto aunt wrote to say it's time now to come and fetch your daughter. Mariko has finished high school and her time is ripe. Besides she's going around pretending that she doesn't have a mother. That really bothered me so Papa scraped enough money together and put me on the next boat to Nippon. Except for baby Irene who came with me I left the other kids in George and Papa's care. George made a list of things they had to do and as big brother he made sure they did their share.

When we arrived in Yokohama we stayed over with a distant cousin who turned out to be the madam of a prostitution house.[1] Now from the street her place looked like any inn you could find on a busy sidestreet but as soon as I stepped inside and made my presence known I knew the kind of place it was. Just inside the entranceway there was a wall full of glossy nudes. The customers would step in and after nodding to the madam look intently at the pin-ups. When they made up their minds which girl they wanted to bed down with they informed the madam and paid up front. We slept right next to one of the rooms they made love in. The walls were paper thin. One night we heard a young girl cry out NO! NO! I DON'T WANT TO! I DON'T WANT TO! I felt sorry for her but what could I do? I was only a guest in the house of life myself.

Poor girls from the countryside often get enticed by the night-life of the big cities. Who knows how many of them end up selling their bodies. One way or another they have to make ends meet. It was that way in the past and it's still that way today. Even in Edmonton along Whyte Avenue you can catch attractive girls showing off their bodies and all kinds of men in sleek cars pulling up at the curb before whisking them away.

I heard from one of my old Tosa friends that the latest move on the part of the city fathers had to do with giving the world's oldest profession a facelift. Ha! Now most Japanese live in small homes packed close together and nobody but a monk in his mountain hideaway has the kind of privacy we take for granted over here. So lots of night-life spills onto the streets and needless to say the Gay Quarters are an invitation to forego your daily woes. That's why the Love Hotels Spas and Houses of Pleasure flourish in all the cities. Fashions are here today and gone tomorrow but the sexual appetite goes on flowing unabated through the city streets. Young men who wouldn't think of sleeping with their girlfriends still have their sexual initiation at a brothel. Old merchants with a fat wallet still take pride in keeping a geisha. When it comes to the "loving game" yesterday today and tomorrow are all the same.

You know when Papa returned to Nippon all those years ago to find himself a wife he paid a visit to the Yoshiwara district which in its heyday was Kyoto's famous Red Light District. Papa said that most of the girls were exhibited in bamboo cages like animals in a zoo. He didn't say that he felt disgusted and I didn't ask him if the sight of naked women cooped-up in bamboo cages honed his appetite. It was after all none of my business. That he told me as much as he did surprised me. I don't know if he went to brothels after our marriage. I suspect he did but not very often because I knew he couldn't afford it. His drinking was enough to keep us broke.

Well when I got back to Kyoto in 1938 Mariko was still living in Furukawa-cho with my aunt and uncle. Now despite all the years we'd been parted I still felt I was her mother. After all who else worried themselves sick about her across an ocean? But as soon as we met it was clear to each of us we could never play the part of a respectable mother and a dutiful daughter. Still we made the most of it and I suppose you could say that as mother and daughter we got along.

Apparently she had told her school friends that both her parents were dead. Imagine that! Anyhow I met one of her high school teachers who said that she could tell those kids who had lost a loved one by their sad faces but she couldn't take Mariko's bereftment seriously because she seldom wore a sad face.

On another occasion Mariko and I got together with some of her high school friends for afternoon tea on Kawaramachi. When they saw us sitting side by side they all remarked O Mariko you have a lovely mother! Why did you tell us she was dead? Why did you pull the wool over our eyes? We all had a good laugh on Mariko that afternoon and she took it on the chin with a sly smile knowing that we were all fond of her. In her fantasies she must have liked playing the part of a "li'l orphan Annie" and to do that she had to consign Papa and me to the realm of Hungry Ghosts.

Leaving George and Mariko with their grandparents wasn't my desire. It wasn't an easy thing to do but it was ordinary. Papa and I didn't make up the rules. I've had to tell her many times that it really wasn't "personal." But by the time she finally joined us after the war it was too late to make amends. Now nothing can be done about it. O I tell you even if you don't have a cent to your name don't ask others even your kin to look after your kids because you'll pay for it like I have. To this day I feel a big gap between us when we're together.

Still it was good to be in touch with her at last and it was doubly good living with my aunt and uncle again in Furukawa-cho. I felt everything Japanese welling up in me. Irene started to walk and even speak a bit of kansai-ben. Mariko and I couldn't make up for all the lost years but we became good friends. Then in 1940 a letter arrived from Papa saying I ought to hurry home because talk of a Pacific War was spreading and if I didn't book my passage I might be stuck in Nippon.

I was reluctant to leave but I knew it was time to return for Papa, George and the other kids' sake. I hoped Mariko would come with me. After all that was the plan. But Mariko was now an adult with her own plans and as she said Kyoto was her true bailiwick. So I left her there and sailed back with Irene.

Notes:

1 Roy's sister Mariko recalls that their mother was met at Yokahama by a relative and that they then stayed at House Yamato, the house of an acquaintance in the red light district of Tokyo.

l'aura of the Ukraine Opal Alberta the

Caroniferous Sky over Europa. and Asia: Black
as my horse Sleepy Jim who fell thru
the winter sod roof of our Root Cellar & ate ate
til the snow the Snow falling thru the hole
the huge Sky-hole he had fallen thru fell down on
top of him: Black as his bloated-belly his
Nest of masht-up roots. we tore out the whole front
of the cellar to bruise him an exit—
and chained behind the tractor dragged Jim thru

  aphasia a cross the frozen stubble
  aphasia of his Famine
  aphasia the drifting snow-mantl'd pasture broke n
  aphasia down the huge hole
  aphasia Black . root . **pie** *in the sky*

  aphasia . . . .

from *the Fontainebleau Dream Machine* (1977)

Part Five

A Bitter Pill to Swallow

By the time the Second World War broke out in Europe Papa and I and the kids had been in Calgary for over ten years. Most of our neighbours were immigrants from England and Europe. We visited back and forth and shared all manner of things in a patchwork quilt kind of English our children would grow up to be ashamed of. We all had enough to eat and lots of water for dishes and a bath. Best of all nobody in a brown uniform knocked on the door to tell us to pull our nightshades down and keep our children indoors and our doors locked.

But when the Japanese bombed Pearl Harbour and the newspapers began calling us "Japs" all this neighbourliness started to change. Some of our friends began avoiding us. Others turned away without a hullo if we met on the sidewalk. The last straw was when our kids came running home from school with tear-filled eyes because all their buddies began turning away from them and they didn't know why.

It was different during the First World War. The Japanese military had formed an alliance with the British so we Issei felt optimistic about our Canadian future. When I came over along with countless picture brides, you could say we came on the glad tidings of that alliance. If you happen to be an immigrant family who wants to get ahead it's always reassuring to be on the winner's side.

But during the Second World War the Japanese military aligned themselves with the Germans and Italians and this time around the British and Americans looked down on us as their mortal enemy. O it was dismaying to be called a JAP just when we were beginning to feel Canadian and most of us had Canadian citizenships and passports.

Still there were many white people who went out of their way to befriend us. They could see that Papa and I didn't have anything to do with the war in Asia. The manager of the Carlton was one of them. He was a fair-minded guy and more than willing to keep Papa on but the owners told him it wouldn't be good for business to have a Jap up front so he reluctantly let Papa go. After that the two of them went on sharing local politics over a beer in the Carlton pub.

Most Issei men of Papa's generation spent their lives working in hotels but after Pearl Harbour they all lost their jobs. Now there was no work left for Papa, George and the others in Calgary. What were we supposed to do with six hungry mouths to feed? Papa began to drink too much and left us even more penniless. George tried to enlist in the Canadian Army but the local military wouldn't have him though he was a Canadian citizen.

We Issei families who had lived all over the prairies since the twenties didn't get shoved into Relocation Camps. But we did get fingerprinted and registered as "Enemy Aliens" just like all the Japanese-Canadians on the West Coast. Like them we were deprived of both freedom and livelihood. Twenty-five years after coming to Canada and becoming citizens we were stripped of everything. Boy it's been a bitter pill to swallow.

The spring after Pearl Harbour we got the kids and all the things we could carry with us on the train and headed for Opal, a village north of Edmonton. It was where our friends the Watanabes had invited us to come if things got out of hand. At first we lived in a log house with a sod roof. Then we lived in a small two-storey log house in town until we moved onto the farm. We didn't have electricity, water or a toilet in these places. You could say it was the bare bones of a life but we had enough to eat and all the kids were doing well in the local public school. Most of the farmers around

Opal were from the Ukraine. When we moved onto the farm they showed us how to take care of animals and how to hitch them to the plough and harrow. From their women I learned how to bake bread, make a good beet soup, chop off a chicken's head and pluck its feathers. We got invited to their weddings and pitched in when they put up a brand new barn. Everybody helped out at harvest time. We felt at home in all sorts of ways and a part of us wanted to stay on but the war finally ended and all the kids except Irene, the last one, left home. Papa and I didn't have the will to farm by ourselves so we sold the farm for a pittance and moved to Edmonton.

Papa who had staked everything on becoming a good Canadian got hurt by the war more than I did. Others we knew never got over it. We knew an Issei couple who had raised eight kids on a sugar beet farm after they'd been relocated against their will. The husband was a hard-working guy who got drunk as often as he could and then turned on his family. Disgusted with his raves and rants the boys when they got older jumped him one night and dragged him out of doors. There they kicked and beat him and left him for dead in a beet field. Ah but he was a tough old bird and he survived their beating. He made his way to the nearest town and after cleaning up caught the first bus west and headed for the Interior. He got off in the Kootenays and got work in a pulp mill and didn't go home for ten years.

Ten years is a long time. The family had given him up for dead. Then he quit his job and with a fat wallet took the bus home. Those of the kids who were too young to recall his drunken ways greeted him like a long-lost parent. The older ones who had beaten him up had left home and had families of their own. The oldest daughter who really understood his embitterment greeted him in tears and promptly served him a hot meal. His wife was away visiting relatives in Nippon but the day before she came home he got himself a bottle of whisky and put poison in it and drank till his hands fell limp. It was the wife who found him slumped on the floor with his tongue hanging out. He left a note that said, The midnight sky that nursed my long-ago bruises invites me home. You have suffered as much as me but you were made of sterner stuff.

It's an awful truth but there were many Issei who were beaten to death by the furies unleashed by war. Let's say we were scarred for life. I know that Papa never forgave that man's wife and her kids for their terrible indiscretions. Havoc wears a human face.

It's the Japanese Canadians who lived on the West Coast before Pearl Harbour who happen to be the real force behind the Redress Movement. Those of us who lived all over the prairies in small communities couldn't put a face to the hatred we felt but we knew its ugliness by heart. Then after Pearl Harbour and later Hiroshima lots of Issei really did feel humiliated and said shikataganai [it can't be helped] even as they went about patching their broken lives together. Now given all the unspoken anger and all the heartache it's small comfort knowing that we're going to be compensated. I mean no amount of money can make up for an immigrant's dream gone awry. And if we're compensated will the federal government compensate the Chinese who had to pay such a humiliating Head Tax? Will they compensate all the Native People who have been treated much worse than us?

Those war years were awful times for Mariko too. Papa and I didn't know much about her travails because there was hardly any mail coming through and what did get through got censored. Over the years she has told me many times how Auntie had to empty out all her cupboards just to keep hunger at bay. Even farmers who could usually count on having full bellies had to ration themselves because the military confiscated most of their rice. Fortunately Kyoto didn't get bombed like the other cities but the harshness of living hand-to-mouth left an indelible mark on everyone's brow. By the time the Americans began bombing Japanese cities Mariko had been sent up to Hokkaido by my aunt and uncle to help a relative who lost his sons in the Sino-Japanese war. She said it was touch and go. Bombs were falling all over the place. She got on the train in Amori with only the clothes on her back. The train was full of wounded soldiers. Pretending to be an invalid herself she made it back to Kyoto. A famished Kyoto. O I have no doubt that Mariko of all my kids has had the hardest life and a part of me says I'm to blame.

After the war and then its humiliating defeat she took leave of the Yoshimuras. She didn't tell them where she was going but asked them not to worry because she knew how to take care of herself. She disappeared for several years.

In '62 Papa and I went to Kyoto intent on finding her. We placed an ad in the local paper with her picture in it. The ad said Issei couple from Canada are looking for their daughter. Would anyone knowing of her wheabouts get in touch. Well Mariko saw the ad that afternoon and phoned to tell us she was alive and well. The next day I went to the address she gave me and found her living in a dingy walk-up apartment.

Because Papa and I were going on to Kochi, she came along with us. We got her a small apartment there with everything she needed including a sewing machine so she could pursue her career as a seamstress. What else could we do? She didn't want to come to Canada with Papa and me. She said Thank you for caring enough to find me. I'll keep in touch. Though Papa and I were crestfallen we wished her well and left her in the heart of Kochi.

When she eventually joined us she was forty-plus and a lot of water had flowed under the bridge. O I still remember the day she arrived in Edmonton. When she opened her mouth to say hullo to me all her gold teeth shone. Before the war those who could afford it had their bad teeth replaced with gold ones. Even their fillings were gold. Not to mention solid gold caps. It was like carrying a bank account around in your mouth. Ha! I felt embarrassed for her because such a display was in bad taste in Canada. At least that's what I thought but I soon found out it didn't mean the same thing to her. It had something to do with her notion of beauty.

Sometimes she still whines, if I had known Edmonton was such a bumpkin place I wouldn't have come. It's all the years she lived in Furukawa-cho just a saunter away from Kawaramachi that made her a big city woman. When she's lonely I know it's because she still misses Kyoto. So I tell her you can go back any time you want to but the truth is she hasn't much left to go back to. She doesn't say too much about the old days any more but her silences say a lot.

I understand how she feels. After a long lifetime in Canada I still miss Tosa. I love Tosa so much it pains me to think I'll never walk the streets of my old neighbourhood again. It isn't only me who feels that way. Many Issei still feel that way about their birthplace. I know that feeling well. There are places in Canada so bleak the heart just wants to go to sleep.

After the war and our move to Edmonton Papa was getting on but he still wanted to earn his keep. He looked at the daily want ads and walked all over town looking for work. He felt luckless and as usual drank too much. Just as things began to look hopeless his luck turned. The boss of the garment factory happened to be a Jewish guy who looked him in the eye and said I don't care how old you are, can you do a good day's work? Papa worked at the Toni Lynn till he was into his late seventies.

I got a job there too and worked till I was into my seventies. Most of the women working the treadle were recent immigrants from Eastern Europe. There were a few East Indian women plus Philipinos Taiwanese Koreans and me. O you should have heard us chattering in our pidgin-English over lunch. We all knew what poverty and pushing the treadle meant and we were grateful for the privilege of earning our keep. Plus we got to take home our share of spoiled clothes. For years I dipped into one cardboard box or another to put a skirt, a blouse or sweater on a grandchild's back. The Toni Lynn paid only minimum wages and worked us hard but they didn't debase us. Years after Papa and I stopped working there we still used to get a Christmas card from the boss wishing us a Happy New Year.

Now Papa always wanted George to marry a Japanese girl and when the time came George did marry a Nisei girl he met while working on the sugar beet farms in southern Alberta. So you could say a part of Papa's plan worked out. But all the other kids grew up and went out into the world and one by one fell in love with white people. Papa and I knew it couldn't be helped. After all their friends were white kids. Anyhow Papa couldn't say no to them though I know a part of him couldn't say yes.

Take Franky our youngest son who went off to Denmark on a graduate scholarship. On his way home he met a Scottish girl who was coming to Edmonton to take up a nursing job. They were on the same train and by the time it arrived in Edmonton they knew they liked each other. It turned out Ann didn't know a soul in Edmonton so at Franky's insistence we let Ann stay in the basement room until she found her own place.[1] Papa didn't like the idea but Franky was his pet so he didn't say no. Well soon after that Franky and Ann got married. Papa was a bit skeptical about the marriage. He had a thing about Catholics and told Franky it would only lead to trouble if he married one.[2] Franky reassured Papa that he had no intention of becoming a Catholic and so Papa gave them his blessing. Franky and Ann didn't care for big city life so they moved out to the country, to Hinton where Franky taught phys-ed in the local school and made pots in his spare time. The two of them had three kids of their own and then to our amazement they adopted a Korean child and named him Sumio. Modern couples like Ann and Frank tell their adopted child where he came from as soon as the child can understand.[3] Sumio knows he was an abandoned baby but we really don't know how he feels about it. I suppose that'll always be his secret.

As far as marriage went it was the same for both Roy and Harry. Apart from their sisters they didn't know many Japanese girls when they were growing up so they fell in love with white girls. And George's oldest son Cliff fell in love with a French-Canadian girl he met at Jasper. They got married a few months after Papa passed away.

You see there was just a scattering of us across the prairies in the early years. In most prairie towns we were barely a community. When Papa and I took leave of Victoria in the early twenties we were never again a part of the larger JC community. That's how it was for us Issei who lived on the prairies. Then after Pearl Harbour the numbers of JCs increased till those of us who had lived in one small town or another since the twenties found ourselves at odds with all those who came from B.C. with their loyalties intact. It's funny how the local politicians lumped us all together in the name of an ersatz community we never felt wholly a part of.

Anyhow, Roy was working as a window display man at the Parisienne and teaching nights at the art school in Calgary and that's where he and Monica first got together. She worked in the town planning department in City Hall. In the beginning her parents thought of Roy as a bright young guy and a fledgling artist and invited him up for tea. Things were cordial enough until the night he asked them for Monica's hand. They were taken aback by his brashness and told him bluntly they hadn't brought up their only daughter to marry an Asian. Monica wanted to be out on her own and Roy was nearly thirty. So over her parents' heated objections they got married.

For several years after that Monica's parents wouldn't have anything to do with them. But when Roy and Monica moved out to Vancouver they came out one summer because they were curious about their three grandchildren. They didn't come to the house. No, they waited for Monica and the kids in Stanley Park where they spent the afternoon together. It was the kids that brought them around. But as far as Roy was concerned their rejection of him couldn't be mended.

Then there's the other side of the story. When Roy came up to Edmonton one weekend to tell Papa and me they were going to get married Papa was upset. Why didn't you tell me you wanted to get married? he said, I would have found a Japanese woman for you. He didn't want to believe they had made up their minds but in the end he gave them his blessing. Anyhow after they got married Papa grew very fond of Monica and praised her for her common sense. Years later he was most upset when he found out that the two of them got divorced. Papa wrote Roy and told him tersely that he was a damn fool and that he would never find a better woman. Monica always looks in on me when I'm in Vancouver. Our friendship hasn't changed.

As for Harry, well he's the educated one among my kids. Years ago when he applied for a teaching job in Edmonton the school board told him he was over-qualified. Then he got a job teaching art at the University of Calgary and he's been there ever since. Harry studied more than the other boys. He didn't chase women like Roy did. Harry stayed single till he was forty and then he married Kate Ohe, the sculptor. They don't have a family. Instead they've got a big house full of art and two cats and a big garden to keep them busy. A few times a year I get on the bus to Calgary to spend a week or two with them. On a clear day you can almost touch the snow-capped Rockies from their front door.

Joyce has been unlucky with men. She's been married twice. The first time was to a French-Canadian guy in the Air Force. Papa objected. He said it wasn't because he was French-Canadian, it was because he was the heartless sort who would leave Joyce as soon as he got bored. Anyhow the two of them were married and soon after that Lucien got posted back to his native Quebec and so the two of them moved there. We didn't hear from Joyce for a while but we knew she was working full-time in an English bank to support

Lucien's expensive habits. Then under the pretext that his squadron had been posted to Europe he left without leaving any forwarding address. Several months passed and Joyce didn't hear from him. She finally came back to Edmonton alone and broken-hearted. For many years she held down two jobs to pay off his debts. After seven years she filed for desertion and got her freedom back.

The second time, Joyce got together with a local Nisei guy who used to come around because he was keen on Irene but Irene didn't take a fancy to him so he turned to Joyce. Papa thought this young guy was too much like his own father and even though he didn't say a word to Joyce I know he didn't really approve. As things turned out this guy was a two-bit gambler who spent all his spare time at the horse races but seldom won a penny. Joyce could see what was coming and had it out with him. They were only married for three years. I don't know why my daughters have had such bad luck with men. Maybe it has something to do with being Japanese in a whiteman's world.

I took Irene to Kyoto with me when she was a baby and by the time the two of us returned to Canada she spoke and acted like a Japanese child. But she grew up in Opal Alberta. Papa and I knew she was our last child — after all she was number seven and I was forty-plus. When she finished high school Papa thought she'd make a good pharmacist because there was something fastidious in her but she wasn't a bit interested so we didn't insist. After all she was our baby. She lived at home with us till her late twenties. We used to say Irene you'd better find a good man soon or you'll end up a lonely spinster with no kids and only your old parents to fret over. That's okay Mom, I'm not the mothering kind she says. She's been a career woman all her life. Years ago she said I don't want to end up doing laundry for a man but most of all I don't like the idea of being bossed around. She's always made a good living and kept a nice apartment full of art. Though she's missed out on one of life's big experiences she's got lots of friends and her life is brimful.

O it's too bad I didn't learn how to read and write English as well as Papa. Papa had a touch of the scholar in him. Plus the Meiji curiosity about North America and Western ways. But I can speak and tell simple things. And I don't let my English get in my way. I've got many English-speaking friends and they don't seem to mind.

Charlie is one of them. He's my son Franky's best friend. Charlie went home to Scotland for visits and when he came back with a new bride we threw a big party for the two of them and their friends. Charlie, Joan and the kids are like members of my own family. Charlie phones me regularly to see how I am and to give me his news. In lots of ways he's more thoughtful than my own sons. I've always felt that a man or woman's real nature means more than their skin colour and I'm sure Charlie and Joan feel the same.

Ordinary people and their lives have always held my interest. It was different for Papa, he wasn't one to pry into other people's lives. Live and let live he would say. TV really came into our lives too late to change us. Papa liked to keep an eye on world politics and the hockey games. I liked to knit while watching a soap opera. So we seldom sat and watched the same program. For Papa TV couldn't replace books. Whereas I always wanted to know if the guy playing the part of the nice guy got the nasty guy in the end, not to mention his woman. What are fantasies all about if they don't have a bearing on our commonsense lives?

In our old age we had everything we needed. The boys had their own growing families by then and Papa and I were grandparents many times over. So the seasons passed one by one and we went on abiding each other until Papa quietly passed away on the 8th of March 1974. He was eighty-six.

For some time he had lain in the hospital expecting death to overtake him but all death did was ease the last bit of breath out of him. I don't think Papa died a happy man but I don't really know because happiness was something we never spoke about. He was by inclination the solitary kind and I guess that's why books meant so much to him. The kids remember his face appearing only when he looked up from his book.

Papa never said you should learn to read well because books empower you. No, he didn't say a thing about his reading but I know he passed on the reading habit to the boys. Towards the end I felt a gentle glow coming from him. It was a warmth I had never felt in all our years together.

Anyhow I have a portrait of him as a dapper young man with a cigarette in his hand. It's sitting on my night table and sometimes I talk to him in the middle of the night and even though he doesn't say anything I know he's listening. He was always a good listener.

You know when Papa returned to Kochi all those years ago to find himself a wife he was no longer quite Japanese. There was something haikara [spiffy, "high collar"] in the way he puffed on his cigarette and blew smoke rings. Even the way the tweed cap sat on his head and the way he spoke nihongo had become lopsided. Papa was an oddball and an oddball he remained all his life. At eighty he could still drink men half his age under the table. He kept us poor with his alcoholic ways — Scotch and Irish whiskies brandy and rum not to mention dandelion wine were his constant companions.

Even as he lay dying in the hospital all he wanted was one last drink. I didn't sneak in a bottle because the nurse said it was a no no. But Franky put a few drops of "brandy" in Papa's tea and said, Here Papa have a drink. Papa downed it and turning to Franky said, Now I can die with my thirst quenched but it would be nice to have one last nip to keep me warm. Franky obliged. Towards the end you see Papa lost his taste buds. He couldn't tell whisky from tepid tea. I felt bad because Franky told Papa a lie but I'm sure Papa didn't mind.[4] In his last days Mariko went to the hospital every day and sat with him. She gave him his last thimbleful of "brandy."

You know an odd thing happened to him when he was in the hospital. He started to shout Oi, Come here! in his gruff Tosa-ben whenever he wanted attention. I was embarrassed when I was told about it so I scolded him. I said, Papa this isn't Tosa, this is Canada. You have to speak English if you want attention. Though his eyes were closed he chuckled. The nurse on duty said it was sure funny to hear the old geezer shout, Oi Come here! On his death-bed Papa had all but forgotten his hard-earned English. In his dreams his tongue was wagging back in a bamboo grove in Umagi.

Like I've said he was one of the top graduates from Aki high school. He learned his English there from a Methodist missionary before going off to the new world. In 1962 when we went back to Tosa together he took a big trunkful of English books to donate to his old high school but local politics had changed. Now all the teachers were Communists first and scholars last. So Papa changed his mind and sold the books to a second-hand dealer. He was quite disheartened about that.

I've never learned to read and write English. I was never the bookish type. I suppose if I had been our marriage might have been more congenial. I'm the sort who keeps everything of value stored in their memory — or else tucked away in my steamer trunk.

But then, except for George and Mariko who learned their Japanese in Nippon, all my kids grew up without learning more than the bare necessities of nihongo. It's really too bad but given the fact that we lived entirely in a whiteman's world Papa and I didn't have the time or inclination to teach them. Besides the desire to rid ourselves of our immigrant status was very strong.

I can't say what I really feel in English and my kids can't tell me much about themselves in their broken Japanese. When they say, Mom. . . .? I ask, what-you-want in broken English. My English is simple-minded to them but that's okay because most of the time we don't even know we're mixing broken English and simple-minded Japanese. Things get muddled up but we don't stop talking. It's not a big problem. We all understand that our gestures and silences have their part to play.

Roy speaks an adequate Japanese. When the two of us went to Kochi in '86 he bought all the plane and train tickets and looked after our meals and lodgings. I didn't lift a finger. When the others go they take their pocket dictionaries. Lucky for them they know enough Japanese to get by. George was in Umagi till he was thirteen so he can read and write though he's forgotten a lot. And Mariko spent her first forty years speaking Japanese. These days she spends a lot of time studying English. She's nothing if not diligent.

It's really too bad we couldn't have taken the time to teach them Japanese. I casually mentioned this to Papa one day. He turned on me and said, It's okay, they're Canadians so English is more important.

I wasn't a very keen student during my school years but two of my best friends were among the honour students. One of them writes to me regularly. She's been going to a college for seniors and learning new things. She stays until three and after tea with fellow students she takes a taxi home. Needless to say she comes from a wealthy family.

My life is just as comfortable as hers though I never take taxis. All my kids are alive and well. I have ten grandchildren and seven great grandchildren, each a small joy. My one concern is to remain clear and live to be a hundred.

I knew a fisherman's wife who brought up a large family but sad to say none of them wanted to care for her in her old age. They placed her in an old-age home where nobody spoke Japanese. She didn't care for the white bread and all the meat but she didn't complain. Imagine raising all those kids only to discover in your old age that not one of them wanted to take care of you. I'm so upset with her kids — they don't seem to understand it's only the heart's affections that really matter.

Recently I had a letter from an old Tosa friend. She told me that one of her younger friends had hanged herself because she was fed up with being treated like an intruder in her own household by her daughter-in-law. My friend said her friend's only son was a big executive and away from home all day and half the night so he couldn't see the grievances between them. The hanged woman left a note saying I never meant to be a nuisance. The next time you see me I'll be that yellow butterfly flitting about in your garden.

You know when I was young I heard of how a Snow Country village dealt with its hunger. The story tells of how the oldest son of the village headman knelt in front of his aged mother and thanked her for all she had done for the family. He reminded her that there was no more rice left in the village store house and because of the long drought there were barely any lentils and that the kids were always hungry. Then bowing he asked his mother for her forgiveness and lifted her up onto his sturdy back and tied her to himself. Then he stepped out into the bitter cold to begin the steep ascent. The snow was pelting the mountain slope. Hours later frostbitten and barely able to lift his feet he reached the windswept ledge just below the pinnacle.

What a sight! The whole ledge was heaped with skeletons. Some were scoured white and clean. Others had bits of hair and skin attached to them. Here the famished son laid his mother down among the wind-wracked bones. Bowing he mumbled a mute prayer on her behalf and without a backward glance began the steep descent. If it hadn't been for the full moon he wouldn't have seen the thin plumes of smoke rising straight up into the mountain air and if it hadn't been for his frozen ears he would have heard all the village children crying out their hunger. Other stories tell of how they ate human flesh. It's what really happened in a mountain village in Northern Honshu.

It's sad to recall but I think there's something similar going on these days. The son doesn't have to bear his parent up a steep mountain any more because there's no such thing as scarcity of food. No, they load their parents and all their belongings into the station wagon and drive them to the nearest old-age home. It's a good recipe for dying from a broken heart. I've known lots of Issei who died without someone to hold their hand. They simply let go because they had nothing left to gladden their hearts. The younger generation don't want to be mindful of the old people around them. And they're not encouraged to feel that way. But old people don't want to spend their last days with other old people. They want to be in hailing distance of their children. They want to see their reflections in the world they'll soon be leaving for good.

Notes:

1 Frank remembers that Ann was met by friends in Edmonton and that he said to her, If you need anyone to talk to, I'm at my Mum and Dad's, here's the phone number. Ten days later, she called to say she would like to see him and, having no car, he walked her to a football game. She was living in nurses' residence at one of the hospitals but stayed overnight once or twice in the basement of his parents' house when it was too late to catch the bus.

2 Frank has no recollection of having such a conversation with his father. "Dad was very open-minded when it came to religion — he encouraged us to be whatever we were going to be."

3 Frank: "About the age of eleven he [Sumio] asked Ann if she could tell him anything about where he came from. We'd saved all the adoption papers in a shoebox and gave that to him. He disappeared into his room for about forty-five minutes, then reappeared with the shoebox and handed it back without a word. We didn't say a word either and that's all he's ever asked."

4 Frank: "He had an unquenchable thirst, nothing pleased him more than to have a good last drink. But the story Mother tells is just not true."

heapt with leaves the midden hides my mirth

mother
i am nothing but this
pod-of-breath
caressing its heapt-up
exuberance/s
nothing if not all
the mud twig
and spittle consonants
the whole air-
borne extravaganza!

mother the nests
we feather at speech's behest

from *Pear Tree Pomes* (1987)

Part Six

Landscape-of-the-Heart

J have an old friend who lives on the far side of town in a seniors' home. One time I visited him and he told me he was fed up with all the bland food. He said if he had to eat macaroni and cheese again he would go on a hunger-strike. I said why don't you complain? After all you pay them well. He said he needed something to complain about but he really wasn't that serious. Well the next time I went to see him I brought along the sushi I'd made and a bottle of sake. He ate the sushi and drank the sake and got drunk. O let my supper be nihonshoku! [Japanese food] he laughed out loud. Many Issei would tell you the same thing, even if they're cold sober. Ah the older I get the more I think "Tosa" dreams me.

I want my kids to keep going back. How else will they know there's a landscape etched on their hearts which got sown in a bamboo grove? There's a landscape-of-the-heart you won't locate in any geography book and I'm not about to let them forget it, not while I'm still alive.

I've offered Roy a plane ticket but he always says No, Mom, not on your pension money. I paid Joyce's airfare when we went. Joyce got furious when she got confused over there and when she got that way it was hard being with her. I usually pay Irene's airfare when we go and I've offered Mariko the money so she could visit her old Kyoto haunts but she always says, No I'm not ready to go yet. There were the war-years in Kyoto and then her harrowing time in Hokkaido. Not to mention an ill-fated love affair. I guess it's for all these reasons she doesn't want to go back but I know she will one day because we all have to face the fact that our past goes on living through us. George seldom ever shows his feelings but since Papa passed away I'm the only one who knows how deeply Umagi got rooted in him.

In '79 I was still strong enough to go to Kochi by myself. Irene and I went back again in '81. Then in '82 Harry and I went together. It was Harry's first visit so I showed him the house I'd lived in where I'd played beside the Otagawa. Roy has been there many times by himself but in '83 we went together. I have a newspaper clipping of that occasion.

But my main reason for going back in those years had to do with my father's stone. I was shown the big stone and the citation inscribed on it and I was informed that a long petition had been sent to the Governor imploring him to hasten the deed for the stone's home. Father's Iai disciples all insisted they were beholden to "Oe sensei" and that they were of one mind when it came to putting up the big stone. The last time I was there they honoured me with a big banquet and put on a display of swordsmanship the likes of which I hadn't seen since I was young. It's been over forty years since Father's stone got planted in my mind's eye and I'm beginning to wonder if it'll stand upright in my lifetime.

The story of this stone began soon after Father passed away and Roy was born. It wasn't on my mind then but Father's disciples had taken it upon themselves to see that Master Oe got properly honoured. The guy then in charge has passed away but he is remembered for having found the appropriate stone. Another guy took over. He has been very diligent but the municipality has been giving him the run-around. You see the issue isn't the stone. It was found a long time ago and put on hold in the temple grounds. No, the real issue has to do with locating the proper site for it.

Several years went by and then one day I got a letter from them saying, You will surely be pleased to know that final arrangements have been made to place Master Oe's stone in the Yamanouchi's family shrine. Given Master Oe's singular relationship to the Yamanouchis we feel that it's a fitting climax to our search. Rest assured that the big stone will be properly sited the next time you come this way. Thus everything seemed to be settled.

Meanwhile my life was to say the least hectic. Time caught me and roughed me up. Then after Harry was born I got a letter from them saying the Yamanouchis had fallen on hard times and had turned the shrine-grounds over to the city. Master Oe's big stone goes on gathering dust in the temple grounds, they wrote. Rest assured we are not giving up. We will find another site.

You see Father was one of the Yamanouchi's trusted guardians and one of the last Iai masters and that's why the name Oe is inscribed in Tosa history. And that's what the fuss over a plot of land is all about. Father couldn't be buried in a common-er's graveyard. No, he had to be with the illustrious ones.

Let me tell you about the big revolt that took place at the height of the Meiji Restoration and my father's part in it. A group of ten rebels who opposed the new order were caught after a hand-to-hand battle and taken to Senshu Kobe where they had to commit seppuku [suicide by disembowelment, also known as hara-kiri] in compliance with the warrior's code of honour. They were on the side of that famous Takeichi-san who committed seppuku in his cell, and they were against Lord Yamanouchi. They were from Tosa and Father knew them. He had drunk sake and matched wits and swords with them at martial art festivals. But as the Yamanouchi's favoured retainer and because he was an excellent swordsman he was ordered to be their "second."

I won't go into all the gory details but as each rebel prostrated himself and committed seppuku, Father had to behead him.

You see when you plunge the short sword into your belly you don't die right away. There's time for much agony. And that's why he had to behead them. He told me the story many times and I listened to it like a boy does. "It was such a pity! Even I felt sorry. They were my friends. They were bidding farewell to each other and saying, Now it's my turn, Good-bye! Good-bye! and then each one would politely ask me to cut off his head. And I had to do it." It took tremendous courage. An ordinary person wouldn't have been able to do this.

By the time the tenth and last rebel was called upon to commit seppuku the local people were so horrified by the bloodletting that they cried out STOP IT! STOP IT! Thus the tenth and last rebel was saved. His name was Doi. Doi-san ran a small inn and became one of Father's drinking buddies. I used to rub Doi-san's shiny bald dome because he told me it would bring me good luck. Father told me that the last grimace he saw on their faces before beheading them still-unnerved him in the dead of night. You see he was just eighteen when he served as their executioner.

Anyway his big stone still lies on its side in the temple grounds, its shoulders covered with dust. The trouble is that the land for it hasn't turned up. It has to be ground consecrated by the Shinto Gods of the Martial Arts. Thus placing Father's stone goes on being put off. I keep telling myself that if it's meant to happen it surely will.

I've been to Kochi a number of times to do what I could. My old Tosa friends think I keep coming back because I want to revisit old haunts with them but the truth is that's the least part of it. No, I save my money and keep going back because I know I have to do my part on my father's behalf.

Towards the end of his days Papa told me I must do more to hasten the placement of Father's stone. Papa even insisted that the kids ought to get together and send all the money that was needed. Do everything you can because your father was a true samurai, Papa said without saying it. I hope it happens so I can die in peace. I'm almost ninety now. It's getting late.

You know when I went back to Kyoto and Kochi in the late thirties my brother was still alive, though both his wife and gifted son had passed away. O it was such a pity about his son. Hiroshi had won a government scholarship to go to Kyoto University. My aunt and uncle called in their tailor and had him fitted for his first suit. They got him his first pair of real leather shoes and a matching school bag. And then three days before classes began he had an attack of acute appendicitis. My brother wrote to say he couldn't get to Kyoto to be at his side but that Mariko had been with him till the very end.

Hiroshi's brother Sumio is alive and doing very well in Siga prefecture. After the war he went off to Kyoto to work as a truck driver for one of the city's big pickle-makers. It didn't take him long to find out how he disliked kow-towing to his superiors so he asked his uncle for a loan to buy a used truck and began his own hauling business. Now he has a brand new house, a big blue Fuso with a body a block long, and he spends fifteen hours every day on the road. His shrewd inaka [country-mouse] wife looks after the bank account and every yen that passes through Sumio's hands. She's mindful of the twins and the value of their virginity, not to mention their pay checques, the contents of the fridge, and a big pen full of stray cats. After supper she and the twins sit on the tatami putting tiny electronic components together while keeping an eye on the TV. In the early morning they drop the bagged components off at the local NEC plant and collect money.

One of the twins got married recently in a stylish ceremony. The other twin will be married next year. Sumio tells me he's up to his ears in debt but what the hell, the Fuso will last a few more years and he'll have done enough hauling to pay for the twins' weddings. Sumio's got his grandfather's grit. He's my last tie to the Oe clan. After we're gone there'll only be Father's stone to tell others who we Oes were.

O I still regret that I couldn't be beside Father when he passed away. My brother said he was at peace with himself when the last breath took him. And with the passing years I've learned to live with my regrets. Given the wide Pacific and all the kids not to mention the lack of money I couldn't make it back but I'm sure he's still watching for me from Mount Sitsuzan just as he promised.

Sumio wrote to tell me he drove down to Kochi to spend a weekend with his foster-parents, the couple who brought him up after my brother died. While he was there he drove up to

Mount Sitsuzan to offer a prayer to his grandfather with whom he had many treasured moments when he was a kid. It's hard to believe that after we're gone the Oes will only be an inscription in the book of memory.

Because I've returned to Tosa so many times all my relatives think that I'm their rich aunt. Ha! they must be joking. I've told them many times I come on the money I save from my old-age pension but they don't believe me because they want to think that I'm their rich Canadian aunt. Aunty! they say, let's all go out to a restaurant for dinner tonight. Ah they're going to treat me I think, but that isn't the case. They order everything they seldom get to eat at home and eat till they're stuffed. Then when the time comes to pay up they go outside and leave me with the bill. Well I guess it all depends on who they think you are. When my kids go to Tosa they go as Canadians so nobody expects these things of them. But when I go it's the other way around. Imagine being treated like a wealthy aunt when you haven't saved a penny in your life!

Mariko has said, Mom it's beyond me why you spent your whole life with a man like Papa. Here you are an old woman and what have you got to show for it? Papa's drinking has left you penniless. I remind her a Meiji woman couldn't take leave of her husband unless he was a complete fool. After all Papa and I were among those who came here to begin a new life and bear witness to each other's foibles. I remind her that being tied to Papa didn't mean losing my own mind. Mariko knows both the Nippon and Canadian side of things so she can be overbearing. All these small conflicts persist in our relationship. Still, when Papa and I went by dog cart to Umagi to begin our married life I'm sure glad I didn't know what the future held in store for me.

You know after his funeral I took out the piece of paper folded in his wallet and read his last words. I didn't expect much. After all Papa was always a man of few words. The letter said, you'll find enough money in my bank account to cover the cost of my funeral and plot. Otherwise I leave you without a debt and hopefully no regrets. That was it so far as it concerned me. Like I said he was a man of few words. But then it went on, if you decide to sell the house make sure that Joyce gets my share of it. I was so shocked when I read this I had to read it twice. I thought the house would be mine when Papa passed away and that Mariko and I would go on living in it. Given Mariko's separation from us and all her wartime deprivations I thought Papa would want to provide for her. But he didn't even mention Mariko in his will.

Anyhow I did sell the house and gave Joyce Papa's share. She used it to put a down-payment on her own home. We lived together for a number of years. It was touch and go because both of us had such strong wills. Now I'm living with Mariko. We have our difficulties but in many ways we do have more in common. I guess fair-mindedness doesn't count when it comes to the heart's affections.

Here people say "Harry" or "Mary" even if they're strangers. We never did that in Tosa. Papa and I never used our given names. He never once called me "Kiyo" and I never called him "Shigekiyo." I called him "Papa" and it soon became his nickname. Our friends would call us "Harry" and "Mary" and we got used to it and in turn we learned to call them "Tom" "Dick" or "Sally." But as for Papa and me, between ourselves we stuck to the old ways.

One day soon after Papa passed away I got a letter from someone I'd gone to school with. Boy it was a big surprise getting a letter from a guy I hadn't thought of in seventy years. Anyhow he had returned to Kochi in his old age and had gone to our old school to look in the register for the names and addressses of former classmates and that's how he knew I'd gone to Canada. It took a long time for his beat-up letter to reach me because he'd addressed it to our pre-war Calgary place.

He had left Tosa before I did and landed in California. It took him a few years of doing odd jobs to work his way across America. He ended up halfway around the world in Boston. There he opened a small Japanese art and craft store and painted oriental versions of the New England landscape. His business prospered. He married a New England woman and had a family. After their children had grown up the two of them returned to Tosa to see his mother and to see if Tosa suited their retirement plans. He said they stayed for a few months at a lovely resort in Tanezaki but she was homesick and so they went back to Boston.

They agreed they each had a right to be buried in a plot of their own choosing and he was free to return to Tosa.

Only those who have woven all the lively and all the sordid moments together know how to die in wonderment, Mr. Inagaki wrote pouring his heart out to me. His letter went on and on about those long ago days when were just kids and what a tomboy I was.

O I can see the two of us dashing down the cobblestone street into the local sweet shop with me pushing him away from the candy shelf because I wanted first choice and he shoving back. He spoke of the part of town the lepers lived in and how we had been admonished to keep our distance from them or else we would find our own flesh hanging down. Nonetheless the two of us wanted to see with our own eyes if such a ghastly-looking human was possible. So we skipped classes one afternoon and went over to their part of town. We stood in the shade on the far side of the square as they came to fetch water from a communal well and we watched as they carried it away with their flesh hanging down. Nobody knew how they got that way but supersitition said they were atoning for some terrible indiscretion in another life. I must have been frightened of them because I long ago forgot about that afternoon. But reading his memories — Inagaki-san wrote such vivid memories — I broke down and wept. When I went back to Tosa I enquired about his whereabouts. His aged mother who had once treated me like her own daughter told me that he had passed away peacefully with the word "Boston" on his lips. Imagine that!

You know George went back to Kochi after retiring from Imperial Oil. He had his own reasons for going back. After all he was thirteen when he came to Canada. In all the years since he had only returned to Umagi-mura once. Anyhow George said he would look into the business of his grand-father's memorial for me. When he came back he said that he had been feted by his grandfather's disciples who told him all the yen required to put the big stone in place had been collected and a long petition signed by emi-nent benefactors had been delivered to the Governor to hasten the deed. When George told me all this my heart sank. I thought Ah Father's stone isn't going to find its rest-ing place while I'm alive. So I wrote a letter to his disciples saying I'm truly grateful for all your efforts on my father's behalf. I'm too old now to go Tosa on my own so I leave the matter in your hands.

George didn't say much about his personal reasons for mak-ing that trip. And though I was certainly curious I knew I couldn't pry it out of him. But from his scant words I got the impression he had a very good time and that he might even retire there.

Meanwhile here I am. Every spring I look forward to my stay in Vancouver. I love Vancouver in the spring because it reminds me of Tosa's springs. Roy and I always have some-thing to talk about so it's never boring. I don't know how he does it but he spends hours every day sitting at his desk beside the study window with nothing but words exploding in his head. Writers are much like hermits. Once in a while they come out of the cave to eat and say Hi. I say don't worry about me. I've got all my knitting needles and balls of wool and all my letter-writing to do. When my eyes get tired I'll curl up and nap.

I've stayed with Roy in so many different houses. Years ago when he started teaching at Regina College he rented a big house on College Avenue. He didn't know it was a haunted house till I told him. One night as I was about to fall asleep in the upstairs guest room the door of the walk-in closet opened and a ghastly grey face floated like a Noh mask into the room and hung in midair near the foot my bed. I wanted to cry out but my throat was as dry as a piece of sandpaper. I pulled my blanket over my head and hoped it would go away. When at last I peeked out the ghastly face had gone back into the closet and the door was closed. I told Roy and he chuckled and said Mom you were tired and you had a bad dream. Your ghost tales belong to another time and place.

Well after that I slept with the night-light on. But then out of curiosity I turned it off one night to see what would happen and sure enough, just as I was about to close my eyes the closet door opened again and this wizened face with a scar across its cheek floated out.

If you encounter a ghost look it straight in the eye to prove that you don't have anything to do with its fate, Father once told me so that's what I did. Believe it or not it went away. Next morning when I told Roy I'd seen the ghost again he didn't really believe me but he did suggest I sleep downstairs with the rest of the family.

When I get up sometimes in the dead-of-night wondering what made me stick it out with Papa, the only answer I come up with is, Look to your progeny, see how proudly they wear the name Kiyooka on their sleeve. For an Issei woman her kids alone speak of the prodigality of life. Does that make sense to you?

Of course it's also true that since the end of the war more and more Japanese Canadians have married into the white-man's world. Just look at the Nisei and Sansei. They may look Japanese but they don't know that part of themselves because they're out of touch with the world their grand-parents hail from. I know that a lot of this happened because the public school system taught them English history and didn't teach them anything about their parents' culture. Even in the twenties Papa and I could see that it was going to be hard but it didn't occur to us that we would have to forego being Japanese. When I pass away there won't be a soul left to tell how the heart-of-Tosa sang in our home behind an English facade.

Appendices

"Papa." Harry Shigekiyo Kiyooka
as a young man.

Papa's Version

[The following was found among Roy's papers. Matsuki Masutani has identified it as a transcript he made of an interview done by a now-unknown interviewer with Harry Shigekiyo Kiyooka (Papa) some time before his death in 1974. Matsuki comments "The interview . . . was conducted in English, by [an] English-speaking interviewer who didn't understand his background well. . . . That was a handicap for Roy's Dad. Listening to the tape, I could sense a kind of strain in him. . . .":]

My father was a government official in Japan. He had the same job for twenty years — what you would call "Mayor" over here. He was elected three times. After I came to Canada there was a project in our village to open up a lumber camp and cart the wood to the coast. To do that you need a good road. My father made it possible to open the road because every little farmer made [contributed land to] the road, you see. My father told my aunt — that's my grandfather's younger sister, she had a lot of land — so you sacrifice a little bit of your land. But of course the government paid for it, part of it, I think.

My village was about five miles inland from the Pacific coast. Of course that road would pass by my family's property too. I don't know how my father did it, but when I went back for the first time — that was ten years later, when I married my wife, you see — my father looked well-to-do. But he was not, because the government gave him so many standing trees to cut, the best trees — a couple of hundred, or thousand, I don't know. That was his payment from the government. My father never did that kind of job before, so he didn't make any money. Rather, he lost money.

Today there's a big nice road from the coast to our village. There was a small-gauge railway running between the two lanes of traffic. I heard that while my wife was there the road was widened to allow two trucks to pass.

My father lost money on the trees because he hired many people to cut them.

My family goes back eight hundred years. My family actually were Shinto priests. When there was a clan war between the Genji and Heikeh, one of my ancestors lost the last battle at Donorra and came to our village, Umagi, on the island of Shikoku. There were a few families named Kiyooka in our village. It means "nice clean hill."

My father spent too much money, sold too much property of our own. Most of it I think he spent to build that road for the government. But, he wasn't any good man. My mother was about fifteen years older than my father. When I went back, my father had sold about half of our property. When I went back a few years ago there was none left.

When I first came to Canada I tried to find any kin [for a] job. It was very hard. You see, when I came to Vancouver first, the next morning I took sick. I ate a crab or lobster and I think that poisoned my stomach. I lay in bed almost three months. I didn't know how to get to the doctor or anybody. I could write and read English, but I couldn't speak it. Before coming to Canada I had only ever seen one white man and that had been a Catholic priest in our village.

My first job was near the present Stanley Park — Robson Street. I went there for housework. I don't know how much I was paid, maybe five or ten dollars a month I guess. One day those people bought a piano and had to move it into the house. They gave me fifty cents for helping to push it into the house. I thought, "Gee, this is big money!"

After that, I worked in the Hotel Vancouver, running the elevator up-down, up-down. It was a very old-fashioned elevator. One day a Japanese boy died in the elevator shaft. He was squeezed like a piece of paper.

Then I went to Victoria. It was 1907. The Empress Hotel wasn't quite finished. I got a job at the Driard Hotel. I went to the whaling station after I'd been in Victoria for a few years.

In those days, I was expected to marry a Japanese woman — especially in my family. So many hundred years, no mixed blood, you see. So my father wrote me to come back and get married.

In those days we couldn't get what was called a British Citizenship paper. You had to stay in Canada ten years to get the paper. I got my paper in 1916 and went back to Japan. That way [it] was easier to bring back a wife. At that time everyone was nice to Japanese because the Japanese fought [alongside] the English and Americans. Japan sent a naval fleet as far as Europe.

My former teacher and my father arranged my marriage. It was arranged in the space of a week or ten days. . . .

Mama was pregnant with George when we were at the whaling station. She went to stay in Victoria and I stayed at the whaling station. I made twenty-five cents an hour at the station. I was working with the whale oil in a factory. I was paid well. Other people were only getting fifteen cents an hour. At times there was no work and then we went to the woods and cut firewood. Or sometimes we'd just make a fire and gamble instead. The men were Chinese and Japanese and there was a lot of gambling. The place was called Rose Harbour and it was in the Queen Charlotte Islands.

Mama stayed in a Japanese boarding-house when she went to Victoria. The prairies were better in some ways than B.C. Japanese had the right to vote there, and the job situation was better. I [first?] went to Calgary in 1909. I worked in a hotel in High River at about that time too.

When the Second World War broke out, I thought it best to move to the countryside because I remembered what had happened in Victoria when the First World War broke out. There was a great deal of vandalism downtown. So I bought a quarter section in Alberta. [Roy][1] was kicked out of Grade Eleven by the teachers and students when the war started. I lost my job as well. [Roy] helped me on the farm for a year or two, then he said, "Daddy, I think I should go to the technical school in Calgary and study painting. That's what I like," he said. At that time it was very hard for a Japanese to get a job. He had a good friend in Calgary and stayed at his place.

Running the farm, I barely made enough to support the family. In the winter I went to a logging camp. The logging camp was run with German and Japanese prisoners. I was the bull-cook. I cooked for about a hundred and fifty men.

I sold the farm a few years after the war. I liked farming, but a small man like me, and getting old — I couldn't do it anymore. After I sold the farm I came to Edmonton and got a job. It was at a chicken hatchery on the south side. That was the first job I got there.

Japan is so different now from how it used to be. I think too much westernization is no good. People nowadays in Japan call their parents Mama and Papa instead of Otosan and Okasan.

Note:

1 The transcript states that George was kicked out of Grade Eleven and that it was George who helped on the farm and then told his father he wanted to study painting in Calgary. These statements apply to Roy, not George. It was Roy who was forced to drop out of high school after Pearl Harbour and it was Roy who stayed on the farm and helped while George, then in his early twenties, worked on other farms farther south in Alberta. After the war, Roy went to the Alberta College of Art in Calgary for training as a painter. All the brothers were interested in art. In 1939 George took a correspondence art course from a Minneapolis college and after that managed a day job at the Palliser Hotel and night classes at the same art college Roy later attended, but George attended before war broke out in the Pacific.

Matsuki Masutani points out that although George was the first-born, because of the long separation from his parents during his childhood and early adolescence in Japan, it was Roy who actually fulfilled the role of eldest son. "Being old-fashioned Japanese, they [his parents] tried to remember the fact that George is biologically 'eldest son.' Hence . . . a confusion." (personal letter May 5, 1997)

We Asian North Americanos:

An unhistorical 'take' on growing up yellow in a white world

for Joy Kogawa & Tamio Wakayama
(read at the Japanese Canadian/Japanese American Symposium in Seattle, May 2nd, 1981)

*E*verytime I look at my face in a mirror I think of how it keeps on changing its features in English tho English is not my mother tongue. Everytime I've been in an argument I've found the terms of my rationale in English pragmatism. Even my anger, not to mention, my rage, has to all intents and pro-poses been shaped by all the gut-level obscenity I picked up away from my mother tongue. And everytime I have tried to express, it must be, affections, it comes out sounding halt. Which thot proposes, that every unspecified emotion I've felt was enfolded in an unspoken Japanese dialect, one which my childhood ears alone, remember. Furthermore, everytime I've broken into my own oftimes unwelcome but salutory silences, I've been left with a tied tongue. All of which tells me that, everytime a word forms on the tip of my tongue, it bears the pulse of an English which is not my mother tongue. There's English "English." There's American "English," pag-ing Dr. Hayakawa. Then, there's our kind of, callit, Canadian "English," not to mention all the other English speaking folks in the rest of the world, regardless of their race, colour, or creed. For good or bad, it's the nearest thing we have to a universal lingua-franca. Unless the ubiquitous computer with its fearsome but cold-blooded logistical games has already usurpt its primacy. Having said all this, I would simply add that none of the above has anything to do with what I can say in my mother tongue.

I am reminded of these grave matters when I go home to visit my mother. She and she alone reminds me of my Japanese self by talking to me in the very language she taught me before I even had the thot of *learning* anything. If there's one thing I can say with a degree of certainty, it's that she did not, could not, teach me to speak English. Let alone, read and write it. After more than half a century in Canada her English is, to say the least, rudimentary. Not that that ever prevented her from speaking her mind. So it is that I find myself going home to keep in touch with my mother tongue and, it must be, the ghost of my father's silences.

Everytime I've been in Japan I've been acutely aware of the fact that my own brand of Japanese is previous to both the 2nd W.W. and television. That in fact it's contemporaneous with that original wireless talking machine, the radio. My more candid Japanese friends tell me that I sound to their ears, a bit old-fashioned. Need I say that I didn't have enough of a handle on my mother tongue to tell them that all the Japanese I know had been distilled in me by the time I was six or seven. Keep in mind that my mother's Japanese was shaped towards the end of the Meiji era and the beginnings of the Taisho era and that's the Japanese she taught me. What has been grafted on down thru the years is, like my mother's English, rudimentary. Right here and now I want to say that there's a part of me that is taken aback by the fact, the ironical fact, that I am telling you all this in English. Which proposes to me that, whatever my true colours, I am to all intents and purposes, a white anglo saxon protestant, with a cleft tongue.

Everytime I find myself talking, talking about anything under or even above and beyond the sun, I feel the very pulse of my thots in a North American/West Coast dialect of the English language with all its tenacious Indo-European roots. Now, concomitant with this recognition is the feeling that when I am most bereft, it's the nameless Jap in me who sings an unsolicited haiku in voluntary confinement. I don't want to go on moanin' the old "yellow peril" blues the rest of my days. Gawd save us all from that fate. For what it's worth I want to say that it's the N.A. Blackman's (African slave) Blues together with the Gaikaku with its grave intonations of an inexorable fate which holds me close to the earth. Talk about our "aural" confabulations. Talk about the soul inherent in the heart-beat (the errant pulse) of a language. One day I want to tell you how music forms a linguistic bridge across the endless chasm of speech. One of these days I'll come by to play my dulcimer.

Everytime I look up at all of you I am astonished by how the very words we go on uttering all the days of our lives, together with all the different modes of silences we gather, like a harbinger, around ourselves, leave their myriad tracings upon your divers faces. I would go so far as to suggest that they have to become an indivisible part of your very postures. I've been talking of how my mother gave me my first language, a language I began to acquire even as I suckled on her breast, and what a motley mode of speaking it's all become in time. Need I say, that she couldn't save me from that fate. But I have seen a look on her face that told me she understood (wordlessly . . .) the ardour of all such displacement. Thus it is that I always speak Japanese when I go home to visit her. More than that I can, for the time being, become almost Japanese. I realize that it's one of the deepest "ties" I have in my whole life.

Here I want to say a few words about my father. He took

pride in the fact that he had been able to shape a mask for the Asian in himself to speak thru, by learning to read, write, and speak a no-nonsense English. He who kept a keen eye on the prairie politics of William Aberhart and the evangelical Social Credit party and spent the spare time he had left over from working his arse off in a garment factory reading. He who tended the flowers in my childhood gardens and prided himself in the fact that he never wore eye glasses thru-out his long life. Lately I've come to realize that I don't really know much about him or how he felt about the shape of his life. It was mostly an unspoken sense of the familial that tied us together. We spoke, when we had the occasion to, in cadences of silence, augmented by simple English or Japanese. I would remind you that the city of Vancouver wasn't much more than a forest clearing when he landed here in '04. Like the typical Asian immigrant of his day he had heard tall tales of a N.A. which was not much more than a mythical wilderness surmounted by a tall gold mountain and a handful of Indians, etc. You all know that hoary story. It's a part of our legacy as erstwhile North Americanos. Anyhow, I must have learned the efficaciousness of silences from him as he was for the most part, a quiet unsurly sort of man.

Now it's taken me all these years to understand the gravity of his silences and to abide the depth of my own and where it might take me. Let me add here that where I'm coming from, silences are the measure of all that remains unconditioned in our lives. My father died of old age in his eighties. For what it's worth I want to say that we took a trip thru Honshu's Backcountry together in 1969. That brief memorable trip was the first and last time we travelled together since my youth. And I've spent a decade trying to see its shape. Write his/our silences. Like everything I've shaped in my life, it isn't what I intended, it isn't quite good enough. Such as it is, it's a homage to him who planted the tree-of-silences inside of me. Such as it is, it's the hard-won language of familial testament.

It's become a "best seller" these days to say that everybody under the sun has roots, a trunk, and branches. That therefore, everybody is rooted in the particulars of their own etymology. Preferences, hence all of our so-called references, tend in the English I've learned, to take these things for granted. For instance, racism, as everybody can and does know it, has something to do with cultural dispositions and, despite all the rhetoric, it has its roots in the language of our fears and is, to all intents and purposes, wholly irrational. Hence our own vulnerableness in the face of it. Nonetheless, I am on the side of those who hold to the minority view that we have to attend to our own pulse and extend our own tenacities. Like they say, "God helps those who help themselves." It's right here that "art" (in any tongue) can and does get into the act: like how do we cause the leaves on the topmost branches of the old family tree to burst into flower, sez it. Sounding all the old homilies (again), I want to insist that everybody is a bona fide member and an activist (each in their own way) in the ongoing histrionics of a given culture. Everybody's "bearing" is in that sense equal, and we N.A. Asians ought to act forthrightly on our own behalf. We shall have to remain vigilant if we are to insert ourselves in the W.A.S.P. scheme of things — albeit their histories. Thank you.

Nov. 21st '75 AD

[from *Kumo/Cloud/s and Sundry Pieces*, Roy Kiyooka, Blue Mule, undated]

Dear Lucy Fumi:
c/o Japanese Canadian Redress Secretariat

$\mathcal{J}$n extended conversations with my mother who is alive and well at 94, we have come up with the following summary concerning my "whereabouts" from 1946 to 1949. You will understand the difficulty of transcribing our interminable conversation in broken Japanese/English, hence this my summary in the form of an attenuated letter. I was but a few months into Grade 10 when Pearl Harbour happened. Needless to say it abruptly ended my education and our plain city life. I had the obscure feeling that something formless dark and stealthy had fallen upon me during my sleep but when I awoke nothing outward seemed to have changed, even though my childhood friends began to fall away from me. I might add that it's a loss I've never fully recovered from. Here I'd like to acknowledge the Flennels who were among the very few Black families in our neighborhood: They took us into their home and hearts during those dwindling months of 1942. To this day I can see myself a gangly lank-haired kid sitting beside a very large Mrs. Flennel at the First Presbyterian Church every Sunday morning. Subsequently, the entire family moved to Opal Alberta a largely Ukrainian farming community an hour north of Edmonton. I spent most of the years 1942 to 1946 there except for off-season work elsewhere. My older brother George spent part of the war years working in huge farms in

Southern Alberta. He met his future bride down there. I being 16 and the next oldest son found myself transformed from an agile city kid with soft hands into an ungainly but tough as nails farm boy: I milked the cows churned the cream fed groomed and harnessed the horses rode the plough walked behind the disc and harrow cut each winter's supply of wood and hauled it home from the govt. wood lot. I helped birth pigs and calves and I helped the hired stallion hump our mares each spring. With an old carpenter's manual I built the two-room log farm house we dwelled in for many seasons. And though both Theatres-of-War seemed comparably remote from the threshing fields of Opal I was moved whenever we received a letter from a war-ravaged Nippon: My older sister Mariko who was born and raised there kept writing to a home she had never seen except in photos to tell about her appalling hardships. And I clearly recall how those precious letters had been slit and the contents scrutinized and stamped by a nameless Censor.

In and through all the ideological strife we avidly attended via the local paper and the radio a small "I" felt as if a punitive fist kept clenching and unclenching behind my back but each time I turned to catch it flexing it would disappear into the unlit corners of our small log house. How could I have known that those fateful years would foreshadow the monstrous years of the Cold War — and now all the hazardous ideological fallout. It's therefore impossible not to see that the "peace" that surpasses our Armageddon mentality goes on being the most arduous of human achievements.

Off season I went into Edmonton and worked around the clock on the killing floor of the Swift Canadian plant. Each day we worked to a quota to feed the ravenous war machine. Each shift I had more than my fill of the outcries of dying animals: the smell of their flayed flesh never completely washed off. Even my street clothes felt tainted. Then in the mid-40s I began going up to the Great Slave Lake to work in the fishing plants. Each summer I was part of a motley crew of seasonal workers comprising WestCoast Japanese fishermen Icelandic and Baltic fishermen and all the First Nations People who were recruited by McInnes Products. Those were truly prodigal Summers. We crossed the Great Slave while the last ice floes stood like ghostly sentinels all around us and we returned to Edmonton in September when the frost-bite night began its icy foreclosure. Lying on my back on a mossy hummock while the Aurora Borealis cascaded across the tundra skies I thought then as now that it was all worth it, that breath itself was the essential gift. I read Hemingway's *Old Man and the Sea* and I readily imagined myself caught up in a kindred elemental struggle. I go on being a part time fish-eater as if their flesh alone could help me atone for all the magnificent trout I had to behead those lean years. *All this and more for less than fifty cents an hour. . . .*

To summarize "I" never set foot outside of Alberta till I went to Toronto the Good in '49/'50. The essential movement those years was between Calgary and Edmonton and somewhat later the North-West Territories. Futhermore I never left Canada till I passed through the American SouthWest on my way to San Miguel Allende, Mexico in 1956. I fell madly in love with and [was] terrified of Mexico and some brazen part of me didn't ever want to return to staid old Kanada. Since then I've lived in all parts of Canada and feel myself quite at home most anywhere. I travel to Nippon and Asia whenever I'm moved to do so. I've got many friends and next of kin scattered throughout Nippon. Europe remains the perennial country of my imagination: "i" keep wondering when I'm finally going to make it over there. . . ?

p/s The enclosed copy of the letter I sent to The Alberta College of Art ought to partially define my whereabouts, between '46 and '49. To this day I would pledge "I" was more an innocent victim than any "yellowperil." To go from "japboy" to "mistersony" inside the timbrels of a lifetime argues a place for mirth in our benumbed lives. . . .

[from *Kumo/Cloud/s and Sundry pieces*, Roy Kiyooka, Blue Mule mini-edition, undated]

Born in Saskatchewan, R o y
K i y o o k a was a respected
poet, painter, photographer,
musician, and teacher. He died
in 1994 at the age of 68 while
working on *Mothertalk*.